The Family Kitchen

A Cookbook For All Occasions

This book should be returned/renewed by the latest date shown above. Overdue items incur charges which prevent self-service renewals. Please contact the library.

Wandsworth Libraries
24 hour Renewal Hotline
01159 293388
www.wandsworth.gov.uk

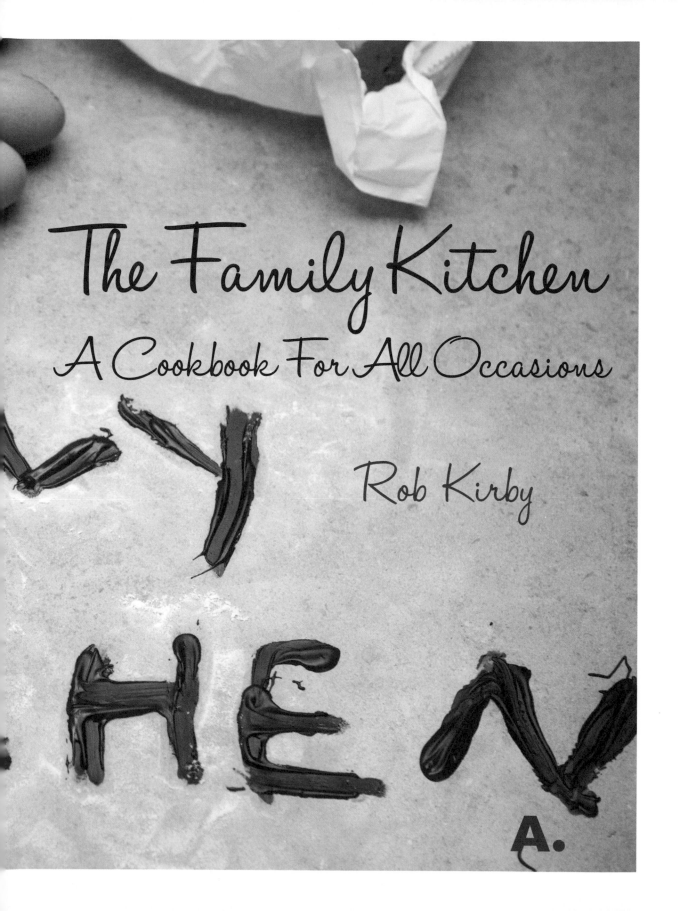

The Family Kitchen

A Cookbook For All Occasions

Rob Kirby

First published in Great Britain
in 2013 by **Absolute Press**,
an imprint of
Bloomsbury Publishing Plc

Absolute Press
Scarborough House
29 James Street West
Bath BA1 2BT
Phone 44 (0) 1225 316013
Fax 44 (0) 1225 445836
E-mail office@absolutepress.co.uk
Website www.absolutepress.co.uk

Text copyright
© Rob Kirby, 2013
Photography copyright
© Lara Holmes, 2013

Publisher
Jon Croft
Commissioning Editor
Meg Avent
Art Direction and Design
Matt Inwood
Project Editor
Alice Gibbs
Editor
Gillian Haslam
Photographer
Lara Holmes
Props Stylist
Katie Cecil
Food Stylists
Rob Kirby and Katie Cecil
Indexer
Ruth Ellis

Cover illustration: Matt Inwood
Interior illustrations: Matt Inwood
and Rhys Kitson

A catalogue record of this book is
available from the British Library

ISBN: 9781906650971

Printed in China.

A note about the text
This book was set using Helvetica
Neue and HaloHandletter. Helvetica
was designed in 1957 by Max
Miedinger of the Swiss-based Haas
foundry. In the early 1980s, Linotype
redrew the entire Helvetica family.
The result was Helvetica Neue.
The first Century typeface was
cut in 1894. HaloHandletter is a
handwritten typeface designed by
Mario Arturo.

Bloomsbury Publishing Plc
50 Bedford Square,
London WC1B 3DP
www.bloomsbury.com

For my very lovely sister,
Elisabeth

Contents

Away & At Play

The Family Entertains

The Family Bakery

Foreword by Gregg Wallace

"I have been involved in the food industry for a very long time, and have been a friend and a fan of Rob Kirby for many more years than I care to mention."

Together we have experienced some joyous (and often noisy) evenings. However, these evenings have always been centred around good food. Not always fine dining, but always good food.

I know Rob to be an excellent and most professional chef and, like me, to be a strong family man.

Both Rob and I agree on the importance and the enormous pleasure of sharing a meal made with love with our families. Smiles, conversation and happy bellies around the kitchen table are some of the finer things in life – things that have absolutely nothing to do with money and everything to do with time well spent.

I love this book. It goes straight to the heart of family togetherness. It is written by a man who, of course, understands food, but also understands the pressures of both time and money that come with looking after a family.

This book is packed not just with great recipes but with brilliant ideas, sound concepts and clever ways of making your money go a little further. We can't all be amazing cooks like Rob, but this book lets us have a go.

A great book, with recipes that really work, written by someone with a passion for food and family. I am very proud to call Rob a friend.

The Family Kitchen

Meet the Family!

Introduction

What a lovely book to write and to follow on from my first book, Cook with Kids, where I wanted to encourage families to get in the kitchen and spend quality time together.

I feel so strongly about the importance of food and how it helps to build a strong foundation for families in today's modern, fast-paced world. It is about getting the kids off their computers, i-Pads, phones and PlayStations and spending time as a family unit, whether it is cooking together or eating together. In 2012 *Cook with Kids* won a coveted World Gourmand award for 'Best Fund Raising, Charity and Community Cookbook in Europe' and it sits in the *Independent* newspaper's list of top ten children's cookbooks. All of this inspired me to write *The Family Kitchen* – I looked into our second-time-around 'jigsaw' family and observed how our modern family works together.

Having worked as a chef for over 30 years, the kitchen has taught me the benefits of structure and discipline, as well as providing some truly colourful, interesting and often challenging times. I can honestly say I wake up in the mornings and still want to get amongst it! With that as a foundation, when things at home were shaken (as happens in most families from time to time), I instilled the same ethos to inspire a strong family bond. When we needed it most, there was only one room in the house that could deliver. Yes, you guessed it – the kitchen! The true engine room of any family.

Our own 'jigsaw' family consists of my gorgeous wife Amber, our children Tabitha, Jasper and Imani, plus Tabitha and Jasper's brother Kerim who often stays at Kirby Towers. Add in Marley the labradoodle and Tina the fish, and you have quite a modern rum mix of ages and characters. Weekends are truly challenging with a lovely-mad-frustrating-rewarding rollercoaster ride of emotions but we wouldn't have it any other way. Truly enriching!

This book started as a long sheet of brown paper that I called my mind map. This was stuck along the length of the wall and over the course of a year, I jotted down all my recipes and ideas, observing our modern family and how it worked, grazed and, most importantly, entertained and partied.

I hope I have encompassed the whole seven-day experience, from everyday quick breakfasts, lunches and budget teas to chilled weekend brunches, barbecues, big Saturday-night entertaining or homemade 'takeaways'.

There's also the Kirby Gift Shop – as a family who likes to visit with something that's close to our hearts, these recipes are some of our favourite handmade and homemade edible presents.

I hope you enjoy this book as much as I did when writing, trialling and testing it. I have given you 30 years of my cooking experience in the 224 pages of this book with some real cheffy twists and turns on comfort food. *The Family Kitchen* is a cookbook for a real twenty-first-century family, where both parents are working hard to keep the family pieced together in a mad, modern, fast-paced world with far too many distractions. So get the whole family around the kitchen table when they are young and years later, even when they have spread their wings, they will keep returning. I can't wait…

Rob x

Above, left: Mini Vicky Kisses, page 194; Jasper's Tastiest Sausage Plait and Beans, page 56

Below: Chocolate-Dipped Honeycomb (page 148)
Opposite page, clockwise from top-left: Jasper's Rack-it-up Slow-Cooked Maple 'n' Jack Daniels Ribs (page 80); Pomegranate Fizz (page 181); Tabitha's Glitter-Bombed Rice Krispie Cakes; Best Ever Cheesy Beans on Toast (page 39);

Introduction

Working Nine to Five

The modern world, where both parents are working is a challenge, to say the least!

Monday morning – deep breath, let the chaos begin! This is where it all starts so I've put together a great collection of recipes that encompasses the whole week, from the early starts to quick, zippy lunches when time is of the essence. Have a go at my Homemade Granola jars (page 23) – they're transportable, easy to unscrew and great for munching on the hoof, whether it's on the school bus, the train to work or in back of the car. Or try the quick-to-make, salty-sweet combo of the Peanut Butter, Banana and Honey Crumpets on page 24 – yum!

In Kirby Towers, it's a bun fight to get to the bathroom first, while the kitchen radio keeps getting moved from Heart to Kiss, and we're all stressing about the day ahead and what it brings. It's a rollercoaster of emotions before we've even left the house. The brekky options in this chapter are special and feature our faves and the ones we eat most. The girls love the Jam Jar Swirlies (page 20), while for me it's my daily fix of Smash-it-up Boiled Eggs on Marmite Toast (page 19). Whatever you choose, these should help you get going and ready for the mad day ahead.

When lunchtime comes, you need something quick, filling and nutritious, like my Shake-it-up Super Salad (page 36) that's filled with orzo pasta, cherry tomatoes, goat's cheese and sunflower seeds or a quick, comforting Best Ever Cheesy Beans on Toast (page 39) when it's a bit wintry outside.

Try sneaking the Do-it-yourself Energy Bars (page 35) into their lunchboxes or schoolbag – they are fantastic, full of goodness and you control exactly what's in them.

Finally, it's the end of the working day – breathe a sigh of relief! Fancy something quick and tasty? Try the Pitta Margherita Pizzas (page 62) for when they come home from school and want something to eat 5 minutes ago! Or throw the All-in-One Chicken Thigh, Chorizo, Butterbean and Pine Nut Pot Roast (page 61) in the oven while you kick off your shoes and have a well-deserved end-of-day glass of vino!

Now it comes to the end of the month, you're eagerly anticipating pay day and money is definitely 'too tight to mention'. Even when you're bit skint, it doesn't mean you have to eat badly. Try Jasper's Tastiest Sausage Plait and Beans (page 56) – banging! Or if you've got a bit of time, make Amber's Egg, Potato and Pea Curry (page 52) with Homemade Naan Breads (page 55) – with such authentic flavours – it's great for anyone in the family at home or trying to live on a budget at uni.

All this brings me nicely to the end of the week for the modern family kitchen – phew! Now, let the good times of the weekend chill begin!

Late-for-the-bus Granola Bars

It doesn't matter how many times we tell the kids to get up, they have to have that extra minute in bed! This inevitably causes angst in an already-rushed household. Make these healthy, chewy breakfast bars in advance and keep the peace.

makes **8** *bars*

125g light muscovado sugar
90g unsalted butter
90g golden syrup (or good-quality clear honey)
175g oats
25g sunflower seeds
25g sesame seeds
25g flaked almonds
25g ground almonds
40g dried pineapple
40g sultanas
25g dried apricots, chopped

Preheat the oven to 160°C/Gas mark 3. Line a 20 x 15cm baking tray with baking parchment.

Slowly melt the sugar, butter and golden syrup in a saucepan over a low heat.

Mix all remaining ingredients together in a large bowl.

Once the sugar and butter mixture has melted, take it off the heat and pour it over the dry ingredients, mixing everything together thoroughly until you have a sticky mix. Pour the mixture into the lined tray, patting it down to an even thickness.

Bake in the oven for 10–15 minutes until the mixture turns golden brown, then remove and allow to cool before cutting.

The Family Kitchen

Smash-it-up Boiled Eggs on Marmite Toast

You either love it or hate it! Admittedly, the family is split on this, but for the many Marmite aficionados among us, this is a winner. In fact, I love this so much I have it for my breakfast nearly every day!

serves **4**

4 free-range eggs
4 thick slices of good-quality white bread
50g butter, at room temperature
Marmite, for spreading

Gently place the eggs in a saucepan of boiling water and boil gently for 5 minutes.

Toast the bread and spread with butter and Marmite, as thick as you like!

Gently peel the eggs and place on top of your warm toast, fork them open, smash and spread evenly over the toast.

Berry Blast Smoothie

I think this is just like me – fresh and invigorating! Tee hee! Or am I just a bit of an old smoothie? A great way to start any day and an excellent way to get some of your five-a-day.

serves **4**

160g strawberries
1 ripe banana
100g raspberries
100ml freshly pressed apple juice
10 ice cubes

Top your strawberries and peel the banana, then place all ingredients into a food blender and blitz them thoroughly. Pour into glasses to serve. It really is as easy as that!

Jam Jar Swirly

In fear of sounding like a family always rushing at breakfast time (that's because we always are), we have these in the fridge ready to go. They are sometimes enjoyed at the bus stop or on the school bus, but preferably in the kitchen so you get your jars back!

serves **4**

500ml thick Greek yoghurt
50ml clear squeezy honey
50ml each of mango purée, blackberry purée and strawberry purée
50g granola topping (see page 23)

Take 4 very clean jam jars with tight-fitting lids.

Pour the yoghurt into a piping bag and snip off a small corner of the bag to give a hole just large enough to pipe the yoghurt through.

Pipe the yoghurt in the bottom of the jar to a depth of 2cm, trying to keep it as level as possible, then squeeze over just enough of the honey to cover the yoghurt. Cover the honey with another 2cm layer of yoghurt, follow with a layer of honey, repeating this process until you get close to the top of the jar. The last layer should be yoghurt, leaving a 2cm gap at the top.

Repeat this process in the remaining jars using the mango purée, then blackberry, then strawberry, separating each fruit layer with another layer of yoghurt.

Top with granola, screw the lid on top and you're ready to go.

The Family Kitchen

Homemade Granola Jars

The beauty of this is you know exactly how much sugar has gone into it! Leave the sugar-laden unhealthy varieties on the shelf where they belong. This is an all-natural seed sensation! Great for the gym bag, school satchels, Dad's briefcase, Mum's work bag, when you're feeling peckish... you get the gist. If you want to rev it up, add a handful of fresh blueberries.

serves **10**

50ml vegetable oil
3 tablespoons water
240ml clear honey

Dry ingredients
300g oats
50g pecans, roughly chopped
50g cashews, roughly chopped
60g flaked almonds
50g pumpkin seeds
50g sunflower seeds
25g sesame seeds
3 teaspoons ground cinnamon

Dried fruits
70g sultanas
50g chopped apricots
50g dried cranberries
50g golden raisins

Preheat the oven to 140ºC/ Gas mark 1. Line 2 baking trays with baking parchment.

Mix all the dry ingredients together in a bowl. Gently warm the oil, water and honey in a small saucepan until mixture becomes runny.

Pour the honey mixture over the dry ingredients and stir thoroughly with a wooden spoon; the mixture will be very sticky. Spread the mixture over the 2 trays, making sure you have a thin, even layer. Bake in the oven for approximately 30 minutes, until golden brown, making sure you turn the mixture every 10 minutes or so.

When you remove the trays from the oven, the mixture will still seem quite soft but as it cools, it will begin to harden. While it is still warm, mix in the dried fruit, then leave to cool.

Once cool, store in an airtight container.

Salty and Sweet Peanut Butter, Banana and Honey Crumpets

My brother-in-law Pete and I fell on these after a heavy night out! There's a salty and sweet thing going on here. These take about 5 minutes to make, start to finish! One of the quickest and nicest tasting things you'll ever make!

serves **4**

4 crumpets
4 tablespoons crunchy peanut butter
2 bananas
4 tablespoons clear honey

Toast the crumpets under the grill until they are golden brown, then spread with peanut butter.

Peel and slice the bananas and lay evenly over the top of the peanut butter. Finally, drizzle with runny honey and run!

"One of the quickest and nicest tasting things you'll ever make!"

The Family Kitchen

Five-a-day Pick & Mix Porridge

This is the food version of an iPod charger! It'll keep everyone's batteries going. It's especially hard to persuade teenagers to eat something healthy in the morning rush out the door; as their fingers naturally inch towards the biscuit tin. Get this down them and rest assured that they've had something decent in their tums to start the day!

These quantities will make more than you need for one breakfast, but the dry mix will keep for weeks.

serves **4**

For the topping mix
25g each of chopped hazelnuts, chopped pecans, shelled and chopped pistachios, pumpkin seeds, chopped dried apricots and chopped dried cranberries

For the porridge
900ml milk
340g porridge oats
4 tablespoons clear honey

Preheat the oven to 160°C/ Gas mark 3.

Place all the nuts and pumpkin seeds on a baking tray and roast in the oven for 10 minutes, then allow to cool. Mix with the dried fruits.

Place the milk and porridge oats in a saucepan, stir together and place over a medium heat for 20 minutes, stirring occasionally.

Bowl up your porridge and spoon over the topping. Finish with a drizzle of honey.

The Family Kitchen

Spanish Tomato Bread

This is a family favourite. We generally have this in the summertime, when the tomatoes are ruby red and bursting with flavour. Also, it's a good use up of an over-abundant crop of them from our greenhouse due to my over-eager planting! Try topping with some Serrano ham – beautiful.

serves **4**

2 tablespoons olive oil
1 large Spanish onion, peeled and chopped
2 garlic cloves, peeled and crushed
500g ripe tomatoes, cored and roughly chopped
1 tablespoon tomato purée
10 basil leaves, roughly chopped
4 x 80g individual ciabatta rolls, cut in half lengthways
sea salt and freshly ground black pepper

Gently heat a tablespoon of oil in a pan, add the onion and sweat for 3 minutes, then add the garlic. Stir in the tomatoes and tomato purée and cook slowly for around 20 minutes, then add the chopped basil.

Using a hand blender, blitz the tomato mixture, leaving it slightly chunky, then season. Allow to cool (this can be kept for a couple of weeks in a preserving jar in the fridge).

Toast the ciabatta on both sides, spoon on the tomato mixture and place it under the grill to warm through. Drizzle with the remaining olive oil and serve.

The Family Kitchen

Funky Frittata

Move over the Med! We Brits are becoming so much more sophisticated in our tastes and ideas with food. I see this in our children, who, even at their age, prefer to opt for a more adventurous lunch. This frittata is great in a lunchbox, when you're eating on the hoof, or served outside with dressed rocket salad and a nice glass of crisp Sauvignon!

serves **4**

2 red peppers
2 green chillies
2 tablespoon red wine vinegar
3 tablespoons olive oil
50g butter
$1/2$ red onion, sliced
200g new potatoes, boiled and
    cut into quarters
2 garlic cloves, finely chopped
6 free-range eggs
100g Parmesan cheese, grated
$1/4$ bunch of flat-leaf parsley,
    roughly chopped
2 x 125g balls of buffalo
    mozzarella, torn into small
    pieces
8 large basil leaves
50g rocket leaves
sea salt and freshly ground black
    pepper

Preheat the oven to 220°C/ Gas mark 7.

Prick the peppers and chillies with a sharp knife and blacken over an open flame or under a hot grill. When they are nicely charred and still hot, place into a bowl and cover with clingfilm. Leave for 10 minutes, then remove the skin and seeds and tear or cut the flesh into thin strips. Place these back into the bowl and marinate in the red wine vinegar and 1 tablespoon of olive oil. Season with salt and pepper.

Heat 1 tablespoon of olive oil and the butter in a small ovenproof frying pan over a medium heat, add the red onion, potatoes and garlic and fry gently until the potatoes start to colour slightly, then add half of the drained marinated peppers and chillies.

Meanwhile, whisk the eggs in a bowl and add the grated Parmesan and half of the chopped parsley leaves.

Pour the egg mixture into the frying pan with the potatoes and peppers. When the egg is just starting to set, place half the torn mozzarella in the pan. Transfer the frying pan into the hot oven for around 5 minutes or until the egg is just set.

Remove from the oven and carefully place the remaining marinated peppers and chillies and mozzarella over the top of the frittata. Place the torn basil, rocket and the remaining parsley in a bowl, dress with the remaining olive oil and season. Pile the leaves in the middle of your frittata and serve.

Pistachio and Cranberry Biscotti

The perfect 'elevenses'! Stick a couple in your lunchbox and enjoy with a good cup of freshly ground, steaming hot coffee – these biscotti are the perfect dunking partner.

makes **20–26**

2 free-range eggs
150g caster sugar
250g plain flour
$\frac{1}{4}$ teaspoon bicarbonate of soda
$\frac{1}{2}$ teaspoon baking powder
pinch of sea salt
75g pistachios, peeled and
   roughly chopped
65g dried cranberries
1 free-range egg, beaten, for
   glazing

Whisk the eggs and sugar together in a bowl until light and fluffy. Sift the flour, bicarbonate of soda, baking powder and salt together into a bowl, then mix this dry combination into the whisked eggs along with the pistachios and cranberries. Mix together thoroughly.

Leave the dough to rest in the fridge for about 1 hour (it should be a bit soft and sticky at this stage).

Preheat the oven to 200°C/ Gas mark 6. Line a large baking tray with baking parchment.

Once the dough has rested, turn it out onto a floured work surface and roll into a rectangle about 28cm long and 5cm wide. Place this onto the lined baking tray and brush with the beaten egg.

Bake in the oven for 20 minutes, then check by inserting a skewer into the centre – if it comes out clean, then it's cooked. Leave to cool on the baking tray. Reduce the oven temperature to 170°C/Gas mark $3\frac{1}{2}$.

When cool, cut into 1cm-thick slices and lay flat on the baking tray. Bake for a second time for 15–20 minutes until golden brown, turning halfway through the cooking time.

Once baked, leave to cool on the baking tray. The biscotti should be lovely and crunchy, perfect with a Sunday morning coffee!

The Family Kitchen

Marbled Banana and Nutella Loaf

Nutella is a constant fixture on the shopping list in our house, along with bananas that never seem to get eaten! Banana and chocolate are an absolute marriage of flavours. This is our lovely Imani's recipe – she's our cheeky little chocolate fiend. This is a great lunchbox treat, although occasionally she can be seen running for the bus with a slice of this in hand...

serves **8-10**

4 very ripe bananas
15g fresh yeast or 2 x 7g dried
   yeast sachets
4 tablespoons runny honey
500g strong white flour
1 teaspoon sea salt
1 tablespoon sugar
200g jar of Nutella
oil, for greasing

Blend 2 of the bananas in a food processor or mash with a fork until smooth. Pour the banana mixture into a measuring jug and top up with warm water until you have 350ml liquid. Add in the yeast and 2 tablespoons of the honey, then stir until dissolved. Cover and leave in a warm place for 10–15 minutes or until the mixture and yeast start to bubble and come alive.

Sift the flour, salt and sugar into a large mixing bowl. Make a well in the centre, then pour in the banana mixture. Use your hands to start to mix the flour and liquid together – this will be very sticky to begin with, but will gradually start to come together to form a nice dough.

Lightly flour a work surface, then turn the dough out and knead for at least 5 minutes until you have smooth, silky dough.

Lightly flour a mixing bowl, place the dough into the bowl and sprinkle a little more flour over the top. Cover the bowl with clingfilm and leave to prove in a warm place for about 30 minutes or until the dough has doubled in size.

Once the dough has proved, turn out onto a lightly floured work surface. Using a rolling pin, roll into a 45 x 30cm rectangle. Using a palette knife, generously spread Nutella all over the dough, making sure you leave a 2cm gap all around the edges. Peel the remaining bananas, slice thinly, then layer evenly over the Nutella-covered dough.

Carefully roll your dough to form a long sausage-shaped Swiss roll and place on a well-oiled baking tray lined with baking parchment. Cover with clingfilm and leave in a warm place again until it has doubled in size (this should take around 20–30 minutes).

Preheat the oven to 180°C/ Gas mark 4.

Remove the clingfilm. Using a pair of scissors carefully make small incisions into the top of the loaf. Bake in the preheated oven for 25–30 minutes or until golden.

Remove from oven, drizzle and brush with the remaining 2 tablespoons of honey to give the loaf a sticky glaze and leave to cool.

Raw Spring Veggie Bites with Hummus

This is great made up in advance so the family can help themselves to a lovely garlicky dollop in their lunchbox.
The sweetness of the onion works really well. It's nutritious and loved by our now health-conscious girls! It's great for picnics too.

serves **4**

1 tablespoon vegetable oil
1 onion, sliced
1 tablespoon caster sugar
400g tin of chickpeas, drained
1 tablespoon tahini paste
2 garlic cloves, chopped
juice of $\frac{1}{2}$ lemon
125ml olive oil
16 breakfast radishes
16 baby carrots or Chantenay
   carrots
sea salt and freshly ground black
   pepper

Warm a saucepan on the hob, then add the oil, sliced onions and caster sugar. Slowly cook for around 20 minutes, allowing the onions to caramelise and become golden brown. Allow to cool.

Place the chickpeas, tahini paste, garlic, lemon juice and seasoning in a blender. Blend slowly, adding the olive oil to create a smooth consistency. Decant into a bowl and place in the fridge.

Take a glass or teacup, fill half full with the hummus and top with caramelised onions. Push in the radishes and carrots and serve.

"This is great made up in advance so the family can help themselves to a lovely garlicky dollop in their lunchbox."

The Family Kitchen

Do-it-Yourself Energy Bars

Picture this: the alarm hasn't gone off (or you've conveniently snoozed one too many times), your shirt for the day has not been ironed, the P.E. kit isn't ready... So there's not exactly bags of time for a nutritious breakfast. Does this sound familiar? Well, here's our solution, which goes down a treat in the Kirby residence! These energy bars are great and keep well if stored in an airtight jar.

makes **12** bars

190g butter, plus extra for
   greasing
190g unrefined soft brown sugar
170g clear honey
380g porridge oats
90g pumpkin seeds
12g flax seeds
90g goji berries
90g dried blueberries

Preheat the oven to 160°C/Gas mark 3. Grease and line a 30 x 20cm tray with baking parchment.

Place the butter, sugar and honey in a saucepan and heat gently over a medium heat, stirring occasionally, until the butter has melted and the sugar has dissolved. Do not boil the mixture. Remove from the heat.

Place the oats, all the seeds and the berries in a large mixing bowl, then pour in the butter, sugar and honey mixture and stir to combine thoroughly. Spread the mixture evenly in the lined tray, then use a palette knife to press the mixture down firmly (spread a little oil on the palette knife to stop the mixture from sticking).

Place the tray in the preheated oven and bake for 20 minutes or until the top is golden brown. Remove from oven and leave to cool thoroughly in the tray.

Turn out from the tray and cut into bars 10cm long and 4–5cm wide for that instant energy boost, or into smaller pieces to keep you going throughout the day.

Shake-it-up Super Salad

Salad shaker pots are all the rage in the City, where the average lunch 'hour' is around 20 minutes.

serves **4**

For the salad
600g orzo pasta, cooked
160g cherry tomatoes, halved
80g red onion, finely diced
80g pitted black olives, cut in half
60g baby spinach leaves,
    shredded
1/4 bunch of mint, chopped
1/4 bunch of parsley, chopped
2 teaspoons olive oil
sea salt and freshly ground black
    pepper

For the topping
40g rocket leaves
120g goat's cheese, crumbled
40g sunflower seeds

For the dressing
80ml extra-virgin olive oil
40ml freshly squeezed lemon
    juice
2 teaspoons chopped chives

Place all salad ingredients into a mixing bowl, add the olive oil to loosen and season. Place into your shaker container but do not pack too tightly. Place the rocket carefully on top, then lightly crumble over the goat's cheese and top with sunflower seeds.

In a separate bowl, combine the olive oil, lemon juice and chives and season well. Place into a small pot.

When you are ready to eat, add the dressing to your salad, place the lid on top and shake!

The Family Kitchen

Best Ever Cheesy Beans on Toast

Beans on toast is a staple five-minute lunch for many of us, but it needn't be just about emptying a tin of beans into a pan. This simple jazzed-up version is absolutely delicious!

serves **4**

400g tin of baked beans
1 tablespoon Worcestershire sauce
1 tablespoon balsamic vinegar
4 thick slices of white farmhouse bread
25g butter
125g mozzarella bocconcini balls
50g breadcrumbs
50g Parmesan cheese, grated
sea salt and freshly ground black pepper

Preheat the grill.

Warm the beans slowly in a saucepan over a medium heat. Add in the Worcestershire sauce and balsamic vinegar and season.

Toast the bread on both sides until golden brown, butter and spoon the beans on top. Drop the bocconcini on top. Sprinkle on the breadcrumbs and Parmesan and place under a hot grill until brown and crunchy.

"...it needn't be just about emptying a tin of beans into a pan."

Smashed Avocado, Tuna Mayo and Capers on Toast

This recipe takes me back! I practically lived on this as a young chef working in Israel (I used to pinch the avocados straight from the trees in the local kibbutz!). After very long shifts, I needed something quick, tasty, cheap and filling. I needed to be out of the door in quick time, as there was a dance floor with my name on it! Whilst my disco days are relatively few now, when I want something quick and easy to knock up, this is definitely near the top of the list.

serves **4**

1 red onion, finely chopped
200g tin of pole-caught tuna, drained
1 ripe Hass avocado, chopped
50g capers
4 tablespoons mayonnaise
juice of 1/2 lemon
freshly ground black pepper
4 thick slices of farmhouse or sourdough bread

Mix the red onion and flaked tuna in a bowl. Add the avocado to the tuna and gently fold in the capers. Add the mayonnaise and lemon juice and season with lots of black pepper.

Toast the bread and spread the mixture on top.

"...when I want something quick and easy to knock up, this is definitely near the top of the list."

Cheesy Ham Toast with Rocket Salad

This is the perfect ham-and-cheese toasty. I used to serve these at swanky cocktail parties by cutting them into dainty squares and skewering them. The secret to these is to butter the outside of the bread, which gives an amazing golden crisp. Has to be tried to be believed!

serves **4**

100g unsalted butter
8 slices of white bread
8 slices Gruyère or Emmental cheese
4 thick slices of good-quality ham

For the rocket salad
1 tablespoon honey
1 tablespoon olive oil
juice of $\frac{1}{2}$ lemon
125g rocket
sea salt and freshly ground black pepper

Preheat the oven to 180°C/Gas mark 4. Line a baking tray with a sheet of baking parchment.

Butter both sides of each slice of bread, making sure to cover the bread completely, and place on the lined baking tray. On each piece of bread, first layer one slice of cheese, then one of ham and top with another slice of cheese. Place the second slice of buttered bread on top.

Cook in the oven for 8 minutes on each side, until the bread is roasted and golden.

Place the honey, olive oil, lemon juice and seasoning in a bowl and whisk together. Just before serving, add the rocket and pile on top of your toastie.

"I used to serve these at swanky cocktail parties by cutting them into dainty squares and skewering them."

The Family Kitchen

Crunchy Quesadilla Sandwich

Mexican is a street-food fave and it's clear to see why. Sink your teeth into this quick and easy sandwich and you'll soon be a convert if you aren't already. Leave the cream-cheese sarnies to the uninspired and dreary... Pack some flavour and colour into your lunch break!

serves **4**

4 x 20cm tortilla wraps
4 teaspoons olive oil
8 slices of Parma ham
200g mature Cheddar or Gruyère
   cheese, grated
2 green chillies, chopped
4 plum tomatoes, deseeded and
   finely chopped
4 spring onions, finely sliced
$1/4$ bunch of coriander, chopped

Preheat a large frying pan over a medium heat.

Brush one side of each tortilla wrap with 1 teaspoon of olive oil, then turn over and cover with 2 slices of Parma ham.

Sprinkle the grated cheese, chilli, tomato, spring onion and coriander over one half of the tortilla only. Carefully fold the tortilla wrap in half so it makes a half-moon shape and press down slightly.

Place each tortilla in the frying pan and then place something heavy (such as a another frying pan or a heavy plate) on top to press it down. Cook for about 3-4 minutes or until golden brown, then carefully turn over and repeat the process for the other side.

Remove from the pan and cut into halves if you are hungry or into quarters to share. Great served with soured cream, guacamole or some spicy salsa.

All-in-the Pan Pizza

The kids love making fun pizza, which is great as it teaches them how a basic bread dough is made. It's also perfect for students on a budget, is really easy to make, and forgiving for first timers! You can change the toppings to suit your fancy.

serves **4**

For the pizza dough
15g fresh yeast
140ml warm water
250g strong white flour, sifted
$\frac{1}{2}$ teaspoon sugar
pinch of sea salt
1 teaspoon olive oil, to grease
    pan

For the topping
150g shop-bought or homemade
    tomato pizza sauce
50g baby spinach leaves, washed
1 plum tomato, cut into 6 slices
1 x 150g ball of buffalo
    mozzarella
4 free-range eggs

To make the dough, stir the yeast and sugar into the warm water until it has fully dissolved. Mix the flour, salt and yeast mixture together with your hands in a bowl until it forms a dough that easily comes away from the sides of the bowl.

Flour a work surface and knead the dough until it's elastic (around 10 minutes). Place the dough back in the bowl, cover with clingfilm and leave in a warm place to rise until it has doubled in size – this usually takes 20–30 minutes.

Preheat the oven to 200°C/ Gas mark 6. Lightly grease a 30cm metal-handled frying pan with the oil.

Once the dough has risen, place it on a floured work surface and briefly re-knead, rolling into a round that is 5mm thick and will fit into the frying pan.

Spread the tomato sauce over the pizza base and sprinkle with baby spinach and cut plum tomatoes. Tear over the mozzarella and season. Place in the hot oven for 5 minutes, then remove and gently crack the eggs on top.

Place back into the hot oven and cook for 5–10 minutes, until crispy and golden.

Crushed Potato Bubble and Squeak

If you're anything like my wife, who, perhaps due to her Irish heritage, cannot seem to make a roast dinner without enough roast potatoes to feed an army, this is a great and tasty way of using them up. It's also perfect served with any leftover meat. I've used new potatoes in this, but really, leftover roasties are just as tasty.

serves 4

500g new potatoes
50g white Panko breadcrumbs
4 tablespoons olive oil
50g butter
2 onions, finely chopped
1 leek, sliced into 1cm rounds
1/2 savoy cabbage, shredded
100g baby spinach
1 tablespoon vegetable oil
1/2 bunch of flat-leaf parsley, roughly chopped
4 free-range eggs
sea salt and freshly ground black pepper

Preheat the oven to 180°C/Gas mark 4.

Place the new potatoes in a saucepan of salted water and bring to a rolling boil. Boil until three-quarters cooked (around 15 minutes), remove and drain in a colander.

Place the potatoes and breadcrumbs on a roasting tray and lightly crush with the back of a fork. Splash with 2 tablespoons of olive oil, season and place in the oven to crisp and colour for around 10 minutes.

Heat up a frying pan to a high heat with the remaining olive oil. Add the butter and shake until melted. Add the onions and leek and cook for 5 minutes until soft. Add the cabbage and cook for a further 5 minutes until tender. Drop in the spinach and parsley and fold gently together.

Remove from the heat and add the crispy potatoes and breadcrumbs, mix and season. Cover with a lid to keep warm.

Place a frying pan over the heat and add the vegetable oil. Gently crack the eggs into the pan and fry sunny side up.

Take 4 bowls, spoon in the crushed bubble mix, then top with a fried egg!

The Family Kitchen

Sticky Chicken Legs, Corn Strips and Celeriac Slaw

Heavy on the flavour but not on the purse strings! The secret to this recipe is to let the ingredients get to know each other for a few hours! Throw the marinade ingredients in a bag with the chicken legs in the morning before work, or even the night before, and just leave them to marinate. When ready to serve, get out plenty of kitchen roll and dig in!

serves **4**

8 whole chicken legs
1 tablespoon olive oil

For the marinade
3 tablespoons dark brown sugar
1 tablespoon Worcestershire sauce
1 tablespoon cayenne pepper
1 tablespoon garlic powder
1 tablespoon clear honey
2 tablespoons vegetable oil
juice of 1 lemon
sea salt and freshly ground black pepper

For the sweetcorn strips
4 whole ears sweetcorn
50g butter
1 teaspoon rock salt

For the celeriac slaw
$^1/_2$ celeriac
1 red onion, sliced
1 tablespoon white wine vinegar
1 tablespoon caster sugar
4 tablespoons mayonnaise
1 teaspoon grain mustard
$^1/_2$ bunch flat leaf parsley, chopped
sea salt and freshly ground black pepper

Stir all the marinade ingredients together in a bowl and pour into a clean bag. Score the chicken, add it to the bag and mix thoroughly and leave to marinate in the fridge for as long as you've got (24 hours is best, but 4 hours will suffice).

Preheat the oven to 180°C/ Gas mark 4. Oil a baking tray with the olive oil.

Once marinated, place the chicken on the well-oiled tray. Spoon over the remaining marinade. Cook in the oven for 30–40 minutes.

Par-boil the corn in a pan of boiling water for 10 minutes until tender. Cut 4 pieces of foil, each large enough to wrap around one ear of corn. Drain the corn and place on the squares of foil. Dot with the butter and rock salt, wrap the foil up and roast in the oven for a further 10 minutes.

Grate the celeriac into a bowl. Add the sliced onion, vinegar, sugar, mayo, mustard and parsley, stir thoroughly and season to taste.

To finish, remove the foil from the corn and cut down lengthways against the husk, in strips. Pile up the celeriac slaw and sweetcorn strips on plates and serve with the sticky chicken legs.

The Family Kitchen

Crispy Crouton Mince Pie

We have this often as it's a great use-up of packets of mince you've found at the back of the freezer! A super winter-warmer and a crowd pleaser for the whole family.

serves **4**

1 tablespoon vegetable oil
2 onions, chopped
500g best-quality beef mince
400g tin of chopped tomatoes
1 tablespoon tomato purée
1 tablespoon HP Sauce
3 tablespoons plain flour
500ml beef stock
1 sprig of fresh thyme
2 dashes of Worcestershire sauce
sea salt and freshly ground black
    pepper

For the topping
2 tablespoons vegetable oil
50g butter
2 garlic cloves, crushed
4 thick slices of white bread, cut
    into 3cm cubes
$\frac{1}{2}$ bunch of parsley, chopped
rock salt, for seasoning

Place the oil in a large frying pan and heat over a medium heat, add the chopped onions and fry for 3 minutes. Add the mince and fry until the meat is sealed and brown. Stir in the chopped tomatoes, tomato purée and HP Sauce, then dust the top with the flour. Stir in and cook for a further 5 minutes.

Gently stir in the beef stock, add the thyme and cook for a further 45 minutes over a low heat, stirring occasionally. Season and finish with a splash of Worcestershire sauce. Spoon the mince into a pie dish and place to one side.

Preheat the oven to 160°C/ Gas mark 3.

To make the croutons, place a large frying pan over a high heat, add the vegetable oil and then the butter. As the butter starts to melt, add the garlic, then the bread. Toss until the bread turns golden brown, about 2–3 minutes, then add the chopped parsley and rock salt. Spoon on to kitchen paper and drain.

Sprinkle the crunchy croutons over the mince and onions and place in the oven to finish for 10–15 minutes.

Homemade Garam Masala and Curry Powder

In the Kirby household it's all about the flavour, so we prefer to make our own seasonings rather than use shop-bought, as this really makes a difference to the taste. You'll be amazed at the difference and you'll be glad you binned the out-of-date jar you've had at the back of the cupboard for the last couple of years.

My best advice – to make this as easy as possible – is to buy a cheap coffee grinder and only use it for this purpose (otherwise you'll have a very strange-tasting cup of coffee!). For those purists who love to use a bit of elbow grease, a good pestle and mortar will do the job too.

Garam masala

makes **105g**

5g (approximately 2.5cm piece) cinnamon stick
30g coriander seeds
10g each of ground ginger, fennel seeds, cloves, brown cardamom pods and black peppercorns
20g white cumin seeds

Dry fry the spices together in a frying pan on a medium heat for about a minute or so until they release their exotic scents.

Allow to cool, then, get your grinder at the ready and grind, grind, grind on the finest setting. Store in an airtight container and use within a couple of months. Dead easy!

Curry powder

makes **145g**

Whole spices
10g each of fennel seeds, cloves and fenugreek seeds
10g (approximately 5cm piece) cinnamon stick
4–5 bay leaves
35g cumin

Ground spices
10g garlic powder
30g garam masala (handy, as you've just made some – see previous recipe)
15g paprika
5g turmeric
7g chilli powder

Easy peasy – you've done this before! Dry fry the whole spices in a frying pan on a medium heat for about a minute until the spicy aroma fills your nostrils. Allow to cool, then, using your coffee grinder, grind away until it's as fine as you can get it. Mix in your ground spices and store in an airtight container. Use within a couple of months.

Amber's Egg Potato and Pea Curry

This is a delicious, very easy, non-budget-busting recipe that will have the whole family chowing down. It'll keep the veggies in the family happy too! Use the recipes for Homemade Garam Masala and Curry Powder (see page 51) to make this dish a little extra special.

serves **4–6**

50g butter or ghee
3 tablespoons vegetable oil
2 onions, roughly chopped
3 garlic cloves, crushed
400g tin of chopped tomatoes ('own label' is great for this as the expensive ones can be too tomatoey!)
2 large potatoes, peeled and quartered or cut into large chunks
2–3 tablespoons Curry Powder (see page 51)
1 teaspoon sea salt
300ml water
3–4 large free-range eggs, hard boiled, peeled and halved
1–2 heaped tablespoons Garam Masala (see page 51)
150g frozen garden peas
$1/4$ bunch of fresh coriander

To serve
rice
Homemade Naan Bread (see page 55)
onion, tomato and coriander salad

Melt the butter with the oil in a saucepan over a gentle heat, add the onions and garlic, cover with a lid and turn the heat down to the lowest setting. Cook gently for around 35–40 minutes until the onions are sweet and gorgeously caramelised.

Add the tin of chopped tomatoes, raw potatoes and curry powder and salt. Cook over a medium heat without a lid for about 20 minutes, until the potato is cooked through. Add the water – you don't have to use it all, but make your curry to a thick but runny soup consistency.

Add the boiled eggs and gently stir through, then add the garam masala and frozen peas. Gently simmer for 5–10 minutes.

Check the flavour and seasoning. Remove from the heat and garnish with coriander leaves.

Serve with cardamom and caramelised onion rice, homemade naan breads, onion, tomato and coriander salad and you're good to go! A couple of Cobra beers for the grown-ups go down a treat too!

The Family Kitchen

Homemade Naan Bread

These are really easy and fun to make – a great added extra for a special curry night. Baking the naan directly on the oven rack will give it lovely bar marks and make it puff up better. If you want to jazz it up, add some caraway seeds through the mix and brush at the end of cooking with butter or saffron-infused honey.

*makes **4** large or **6** small naans*

150ml milk
2 teaspoons caster sugar
2 teaspoons dried yeast
450g plain flour
$\frac{1}{2}$ teaspoon sea salt
1 teaspoon baking powder
2 tablespoons vegetable oil
150ml plain yoghurt
1 large free-range egg
25g butter, melted

To serve
melted butter or saffron-infused
  honey (optional)

Gently heat the milk in a pan until it reaches around 37°C or is warm to the touch. Remove from the heat and add half the sugar and all the yeast, stir until the yeast has dissolved, then leave in a warm place for around 10 minutes to let the mixture start to work.

Sift the flour, salt and baking powder into a large bowl and add the remaining sugar, the milk and yeast mixture, vegetable oil, yoghurt and the egg. Mix well with your hands until you have a smooth dough.

Tip the dough onto a lightly floured work surface and knead for around 5 minutes until you have a silky elastic dough (this is great exercise!). Rub a little oil into the dough, place back in the mixing bowl and leave to prove in a warm place until doubled in size (this normally takes about 1 hour).

Heat your oven to the highest possible temperature (first making sure your oven racks are nice and clean!).

Once your dough is ready, you will need to knock the air out of it and knead again for a few minutes. Divide the dough into 4 or 6 equal balls. Take one of the dough balls and cover the others with a damp cloth. Roll the ball out on a lightly floured surface to approximately 25cm in length, 13cm at its widest point and around 5mm thick.

Carefully remove the rack from the oven and place the naan directly on it (don't worry – it won't fall through). Immediately return the rack to the oven; the naan should start to puff up after a few minutes. Bake until golden brown, remove from oven and keep warm. Each naan should cook within 4–5 minutes in total. Repeat this process for the other naan breads.

Serve hot. If you wish, brush with warm melted butter or, for real indulgence, with some warm honey infused with saffron just before serving.

Tastiest Sausage Plait and Beans

Dedicated to my lovely son Jasper, who adores this. In the school holidays he insists we make this. It's a great rainy-day tea – I don't know why, but I think it's because it oozes 'comfort grub'. If you've got a bit more time on your hands, wrap the sausage meat in ham or pancetta before encasing in pastry. Bring on the beans!

serves **4-6**

1 tablespoon vegetable oil
1 large onion, chopped
1 leek, finely sliced
300g shop-bought puff pastry
1 free-range egg, for glazing
400g tin of baked beans

For the sausage meat
500g good-quality sausage meat
2 free-range eggs
1 tablespoon seeded mustard
1 teaspoon fresh thyme leaves, chopped
1 tablespoon tomato ketchup
50g white breadcrumbs
sea salt and freshly ground black pepper

Preheat the oven to 180°C/Gas mark 4.

Warm a pan over a medium heat, add the oil, onions and leeks and cook for 5–10 minutes without colouring.

Place the ingredients for the sausage meat in a large bowl, add the leeks and onions and mix together thoroughly.

Roll out the pastry to a thickness of about 5mm and cut 2 rectangles about 30 x 16cm. Place one rectangle on a baking tray. Spoon the sausage meat mixture in a long line down the centre of one of the pastry rectangles.

Using a lattice wheel, firmly press down on the remaining pastry rectangle to cut the lattice. Place the lattice over the sausage meat and press down to seal the edges.

If you don't have a lattice wheel, just take a sharp knife and cut the pastry into 14 strips widthways, each strip 2cm wide. Place your pastry strips across the sausage meat in a criss-cross pattern, making sure to seal the edges.

Gently egg-wash the pastry and cook in the oven for 40–50 minutes until golden brown.

Warm the baked beans and serve alongside a slab of your sausage plait.

"Dedicated to my lovely son Jasper, who adores this. In the school holidays he insists we make this."

The Family Kitchen

All-in-one Shepherd's Pie in Cheesy Jackets

Who doesn't love a bit of shepherd's pie? My guilty pleasure is eating this with baked beans. Don't knock it until you've tried it!

serves **4**

4 large baking potatoes
2 tablespoons olive oil
1 teaspoon rock salt
1 large onion, finely chopped
1 large carrot, finely diced
2 sticks of celery, finely diced
400g best-quality lamb mince
1 tablespoon tomato purée
1 tablespoon HP Sauce
1 tablespoon Worcestershire
  sauce
1 tablespoon plain flour
1 sprig of thyme
450ml lamb or beef stock
80g good-quality mature
  Cheddar, grated
50g butter
sea salt and freshly ground black
  pepper

Preheat the oven to 180°C/ Gas mark 4.

Wash and dry the baking potatoes and place in a bowl with 1 tablespoon of olive oil and the rock salt. Mix to make sure the potatoes are evenly coated, then place on a baking tray and bake in the oven for 1 hour, or until soft in the middle.

Meanwhile, mix the onion, carrot and celery together. Heat a sauté pan with the remaining tablespoon of olive oil, add the chopped vegetables and stir. Cook without colouring for 10 minutes, then turn up the heat and add the mince. Seal and colour for a further 10 minutes, then turn down the heat.

Stir in the tomato purée, HP and Worcestershire sauces, then dust with flour and stir in completely. Add a sprig of thyme and season.

Using another pan, warm the stock and gently pour it over the mince, then stir. Cover and cook gently for 40 minutes, stirring occasionally. Remove the thyme sprig and discard.

Check the potatoes are cooked through, using a skewer or point of knife, then remove them from the oven and leave to stand for 5 minutes.

Cut the potatoes in half lengthways and carefully scoop out the middle into a bowl, keeping the skins to one side. Mash the potato with butter, cheese and seasoning. Place the 8 half-potato skins on a roasting tray and fill with mince until level. Spoon or pipe over the cheesy mash. Place back in the oven to crisp and caramelise.

Serve lined up on a chopping board, family style.

Amber's Street Food Chicken and Rice

This is similar to the Thai version Khao Man Gai, which you will find on many a street vendor's stall in Bangkok. It's a recipe close to my heart as my parents have lived there for many years. The aroma of this will take you straight back to those bustling streets of Bangkok. Great washed down with a nice bottle of Chang or Singha Beer!

serves **4**

25g ginger, chopped
1 garlic bulb, smashed
2 lime leaves
$\frac{1}{2}$ bunch of coriander
2 star anise
1 bunch of spring onions, half smashed and half thinly sliced
1 corn-fed chicken (approx 1kg)
1 teaspoon white pepper
2 chicken stock cubes
280g jasmine rice
1 tablespoon sesame oil
4 bok choy, roughly chopped
$\frac{1}{2}$ cucumber, peeled and sliced
Thai hot chilli sauce

Place the chopped ginger, garlic, lime leaves, half the coriander, star anise and the smashed spring onions in a bowl and bash and bruise with a rolling pin (or use a pestle and mortar, if you have them). Stuff the chicken cavity with this mixture, and season the outside with white pepper.

Bring 4 litres of water to the boil in a pan large enough to hold the chicken and whisk in the stock cubes. Place the chicken in the pan and gently push it under the stock using a large spoon.

Gently boil for 20 minutes, covered with a tight-fitting lid. Remove from the heat, leave the lid on and allow to continue cooking in the cooling stock for 45 minutes. To check that it has cooked thoroughly, pierce the chicken with a sharp knife – the juices should run clear. Carefully transfer the chicken to a large bowl and cover with clingfilm to keep warm.

Put the remaining stock back on the heat and bring to a rolling boil, reducing it by half (this should take around 20 minutes). Meanwhile, bring a large pan of seasoned water to the boil, stir in the rice, return to the boil, cover and simmer for 10 minutes. Drain well and leave to stand.

Pour the sesame oil into a wok and heat gently until it starts to smoke, then add the bok choy and toss until tender.

Tear the cooked chicken into a bowl, add the bok choy and rice and barely cover with stock. Finish with sliced cucumber, thinly sliced spring onions and the remaining coriander leaves. Spoon over the Thai chilli sauce (if you struggle to find this, sweet chilli sauce is a good substitute) and serve.

The Family Kitchen

Easy Peasy Feta, Pea and Pine Nut Risotto

The thing I love about risotto is that you can feed a whole family very cheaply as your main ingredient is a pack of rice! Give the rice a little bit of love and attention and you will create a knockout dinner. Risotto's versatility means it will go with almost anything. This combination of ingredients is my suggestion, but channel your adventurous side – there is a world of ingredients out there! Butternut squash and sage, leftover gammon and peas, salmon and caramelised fennel – the list is endless.

serves **4**

1 litre vegetable stock
2 tablespoons olive oil
1 large onion, finely chopped
3 garlic cloves, crushed
400g risotto rice
250ml white wine
100g frozen peas
80g Greek feta cheese, crumbled
50g butter
30g Parmesan cheese, grated
50g roasted pine nuts
2 tablespoons good-quality
   olive oil
sea salt and freshly ground black
   pepper

Bring the stock to the boil and then keep to one side, simmering gently.

Place 2 tablespoons of the olive oil in a large pan set over a low heat, add the onion and garlic, then cook slowly without colouring for around 10 minutes. Add the rice and continue to stir, then turn up the heat, add the white wine and stir for a further 3 minutes – the wine will start to reduce.

Turn down the heat a little and slowly start to stir in your warm stock. Keep adding a ladle of stock every 2 minutes or so, making sure it is absorbed into the rice before adding more. Repeat this process over 12–16 minutes, by which time your risotto should have a silky, creamy consistency and al dente rice.

Gently stir in the frozen peas and crumbled feta, season and finish with a knob of butter, freshly grated Parmesan, pine nuts and the 2 tablespoons of good-quality olive oil.

All-in-one Chicken Thigh, Chorizo, Butterbean and Pine Nut Pot Roast

This dish is in this chapter as it is so easy. You just throw it all in together – perfect one-pot cooking with no fuss! While this is cooking, pour a nice glass of wine and chat to the family about the day had by all; alternatively get the Hoover out! It's a no-brainer and makes a great weeknight dinner with minimum washing up (a very important factor in our house).

serves **4**

8 boneless chicken thighs
1 teaspoon smoked paprika
2 tablespoons vegetable oil
150g raw baby chorizo (or whole chorizo diced)
1 red onion, finely diced
2 garlic cloves, finely chopped
50g toasted pine nuts
1 sprig of thyme
2 bay leaves
1 bunch of flat-leaf parsley, chopped
400g tin of chopped tomatoes
400g tin of cooked butterbeans, drained
100ml chicken stock
125g fresh cherry tomatoes (red and yellow), halved
sea salt and freshly ground black pepper

Preheat the oven to 190°C/ Gas mark 5.

Heat a large casserole pan or ovenproof saucepan over a high heat.

Sprinkle the chicken with smoked paprika and seasoning. Add 1 tablespoon of oil to the pan and heat until smoking, then add the chicken and brown on all sides.

Remove the chicken from the pan and keep to one side. Dispose of any leftover oil and wipe the pan clean. Reheat the pan, add another tablespoon of vegetable oil, then add the chorizo. When the chorizo starts to release its oil, add the onion, garlic and toasted pine nuts, reduce the heat and cook for about 5 minutes until the onion softens and starts to colour.

Add the thyme, bay leaf and half the chopped parsley to the pan and cook gently for 3 minutes.

Add the tinned tomatoes, butterbeans and chicken stock, bring up to a simmer, then return the chicken to the pan, mix well and increase heat until the liquid is boiling. Cover with a tight-fitting lid and cook in the oven for 35 minutes; after 20 minutes remove the lid and cook uncovered just to let the sauce reduce slightly.

Remove from the oven, stir in the fresh cherry tomatoes and the remaining chopped parsley.

Pitta Margherita Pizza

I think it's the novelty factor of the pittas that makes this such a winner with the younger ones in the family. It's ridiculously quick and easy to make! It's also fun for the kids to choose their own toppings and a good way of getting them to be a bit more adventurous.

serves **4**

4 large pitta breads
2 tablespoons olive oil
1 garlic clove, crushed
100ml pizza sauce (or passata)
300g cherry tomatoes, halved
2 x 125g buffalo mozzarella balls
12 large basil leaves
50g Parmesan cheese, grated
sea salt and freshly ground black
  pepper

Preheat the grill to medium. Line the grill tray with foil.

Place the pitta bread on the grill tray, brush with 1 tablespoon of olive oil and grill on each side for 1–2 minutes until crisp.

Mix the garlic into the sauce, then spread this evenly over the toasted pitta breads. Add the cherry tomato halves, tear over the mozzarella and season. Place back under the hot grill and cook until the mozzarella is golden and melting – this should take 2–3 minutes.

Remove from the grill and finish with a slug of olive oil, the basil leaves and a generous grating of fresh Parmesan.

"I think it's the novelty factor of the pittas that makes this such a winner with the younger ones in the family."

The Family Kitchen

Flash-fried Beef with Long-stem Broccoli

We're always rushing around on weekdays, aren't we? When you're tired, there is a great temptation to get out the takeaway menus rather than slave away over the stove. We've been there, but don't you feel a little bloated and dry throated after all the oil and MSG? This dish is packed with fresh, clean flavours and will take you 20 minutes from start to finish, if you've marinated the steak in advance (otherwise, allow 1 hour).

serves **4**

100g egg noodles
400g frying or rib-eye steak
2 tablespoons soy sauce
2.5cm piece of ginger, peeled and finely chopped
2 garlic cloves, chopped
2 chillies, chopped and deseeded
200g long-stem broccoli
1 tablespoon sesame oil
1 bunch of spring onions, chopped
50g roasted cashew nuts, roughly chopped
$1/2$ bunch of coriander, chopped
1 tablespoon sesame seeds
1 lime
soy sauce, for seasoning

Cut the steak into strips about 1.5cm thick and 3cm long and place in a bowl with soy sauce, ginger, garlic and chilli. Leave to marinate for 1 hour (or overnight in the fridge).

Soak the noodles in a bowl of hot water to soften – this will take around 10 minutes.

Blanch the long-stem broccoli in a pan of salted boiling water for around 2 minutes, then drain in a colander. Refresh under cold water, drain thoroughly and pat dry on kitchen paper.

Heat a wok over a high temperature, add the sesame oil and allow to smoke. Carefully add the beef strips, ginger, garlic and chilli and flash fry for 2 minutes, stirring constantly. Add the blanched broccoli, spring onions and drained noodles and toss for a further 2 minutes. Finish with roasted cashew nuts, chopped coriander, sesame seeds and a squeeze of fresh lime. Season with soy sauce.

Serve with chopsticks and get amongst it!

Rob's Perfect Pot Noodle

If you've got to eat a pot noodle, then make sure it's this one! So fresh and fragrant, and nice and quick for a midweek meal. If you wish, add beef strips instead of chicken, or use both! For a veggie hit, add cubed tofu and use veggie stock. I've served it 'posh', but it tastes just as great served in a mug.

serves **4**

100g fine dried egg noodles
3 chicken stock cubes
5cm piece of fresh ginger, chopped
2 garlic cloves, crushed
$1/2$ chilli, chopped and deseeded
1 stick of lemongrass, chopped and bruised
2 lime leaves
2 tablespoons vegetable oil
50g shiitake mushrooms, sliced
2 bok choy, roughly chopped
450g cooked chicken breasts, finely shredded
100g beansprouts
$1/2$ bunch of spring onions, shredded

For the garnish
fresh coriander
fresh chilli, chopped
$1/2$ lime
glug of soy sauce

Soak the egg noodles in a bowl of hot water for 5 minutes to soften, then drain in a colander and refresh under cold water.

Bring 1 litre of water to the boil in a saucepan, whisk in the stock cubes, add the chopped ginger, garlic, chilli, lemongrass and whole lime leaves, simmer for 10 minutes, then take off the heat and leave to infuse.

Heat a wok over a high heat, then add the oil until smoking and toss in the mushrooms. Cook for 1 minute, then add the bok choy, toss and cook for a further minute, then remove from heat.

Pass the infused chicken stock through a fine sieve into a clean saucepan and bring to a rolling boil.

To assemble your pot noodles, divide the noodles and chicken between 4 pots or bowls, add the mushrooms, bok choy, beansprouts and chopped spring onions. Carefully pour over the hot chicken stock to cover and garnish with fresh coriander and chopped fresh chilli. Drizzle over the lime juice and soy sauce to taste.

"I've served it posh, but it tastes just as great served in a mug."

The Family Kitchen

Big Weekend Chill

The weekend is here, hooray we cry!
In our family, we all have a common goal of
'Work hard Monday–Friday and then chill'.

And that's exactly what we do! Our girls can still be found in their onesies well past noon and even our pet pooch is still comatose on his red chair! This section of the book contains recipes for when you have a bit of time on your hands and you can show the family how much you love them with tasty dishes like my Runny Egg with Pancetta Soldiers (page 68) or something more edgy like the Sweetcorn Fritters with Balsamic-Roasted Tomatoes (page 70). These are great for lazy mornings with the papers and Sunday supplements, and all you've got on your agenda is to chill out and maybe walk the dog.

We always try to have one special brekkie a week. Our kids – Tab, Jazz & Imani – all like an à la carte style breakfast – it's nice to spoil them occasionally! And talking of spoily stuff, you have to try the Deep-fried Duck Eggs with Mushrooms and Parma Ham (page 73) – it's as posh as I go for breakfast. Amber loves kicking this off with a nice glass of sparkles! Into Saturday night and it's time for a bit of rubbish TV, so everyone's crammed on the sofa and we hide their mobiles. We troff down on our homemade takeaways, like my Kirby Fried Buttermilk Chicken (page 89) and one of Amber's faves – Fat Garam Masala Chips with Spicy Mango Mayo (page 88). However, on some Saturday nights we fancy something special and all gather round the table to enjoy Jasper's Rack-it-up Slow-cooked Maple 'n' Jack Daniels Ribs (page 80). We also really love our X-Factor Open Steak Sandwich (page 86), so scrummy and a real Saturday night treat!

Finally, bring on Sunday brunch! Invite the neighbours for Virgin Marys (page 115) and Crackling Pig Sticks with Bramley Apple and Sage Sauce (page 102). Or how about a big deluxe brunch table featuring my Salt-crusted Roast Forerib with Caramelised Shallots and Golden Beets and Hot Horseradish (page 113)? An absolute crowd pleaser is The Ultimate Velvet Macaroni Cheese (page 109), a favourite in the Kirby household. I've also got to big up my Whole-roasted Brie, Roasted Jersey Royals and Crispy Pancetta (page 100) – a real must for any Sunday.

Whatever you cook, you won't be disappointed. These recipes are devoted to the 'big weekend chill' and making everyone in the family feel spoiled with great food. After all, it's why we work so hard, isn't it?

Runny Egg with Pancetta Soldiers

Stunning! Get everyone around the table for some serious dunking. We use Legbar eggs which have a pastel blue shell and the most beautiful sunset-orange yolk. Something magical happens when the pancetta and bread crisp up – you end up with the most naughty fried bread!

serves **4**

8 free-range eggs
4 slices of white bread, medium sliced
16 thin slices of pancetta

Preheat the oven to 180°C/Gas mark 6.

Place eggs gently into a saucepan of boiling water and boil for 3 minutes.

Lightly toast the bread on both sides and allow to cool. Cut off the crusts, then cut the bread into soldiers 2cm wide (approximately 4 per slice).

Wrap the slices of pancetta around your toasted soldiers, line them up on a baking tray and place in the oven for 8–10 minutes until crispy.

Slice the tops off the eggs, then place them back in the egg box with your pancetta soldiers ready for dunking.

"Get everyone around the table for some serious dunking"

The Family Kitchen

Sweetcorn Fritters with Balsamic-Roasted Tomatoes

This is such a lovely breakfast as the combination of the fritters with their lovely sweetness and the tartness of the balsamic tomatoes works really well. This is a Bill Granger-style brekkie, and his restaurants are well worth a visit if you get the chance. If you have some fritters left, they're great topped with crabmeat mixed with coriander, fresh chilli and mayo.

serves **4**

6 plum tomatoes, halved
1 garlic clove, finely sliced
$1/_4$ teaspoon rock salt
$1/_4$ teaspoon fresh thyme leaves
2 tablespoons balsamic vinegar
1 tablespoon Worcestershire
  sauce
2 tablespoons olive oil
80g tinned sweetcorn, drained
1 small bunch of spring onions,
  chopped
freshly ground black pepper

For the batter
245g tinned sweetcorn, drained
1 free-range egg
100g plain flour
$1/_2$ teaspoon baking powder
$1/_2$ teaspoon rock salt
50ml milk

Preheat the oven to 170°C/ Gas mark $3^1/_2$.

Place the tomatoes in a roasting tray and add the garlic, rock salt, thyme, balsamic vinegar and Worcestershire sauce. Gently mix with 1 tablespoon of the olive oil and season with black pepper. Place in the oven and roast for 20–30 minutes until soft and glazed.

Place all the batter ingredients in a food processor and blitz to make a smooth liquid. Transfer the batter to a bowl and fold in the extra 80g of sweetcorn and the spring onions.

Place the remaining tablespoon of olive oil into a frying pan and heat over a high heat for a few minutes until it is just about smoking. When the oil is ready, spoon some batter into the pan using a teaspoon – one teaspoon of batter is just enough to make baby fritters (about the size of a 50-pence piece). Cook them until they are nicely coloured on both sides (about 1 minute for each side), then remove from the pan and drain on kitchen paper. Repeat the process until all the batter is used up.

Serve the tomatoes in a mini saucepan or serving bowl with a stack of the fritters.

The Family Kitchen

Asparagus and Smoked Trout Omelette

As a young, wet-behind-the-ears apprentice chef, this was one of the first omelette dishes I learned. After many attempts, I finally mastered the perfect runny texture of this soft-centred omelette. This is my spin on the Savoy Hotel's classic Eggs Arnold Bennett. Serve them whole in the pan.

serves **4**

175g asparagus, trimmed
8 large free-range eggs
1/2 bunch of dill, chopped
50g butter
2 fillets of smoked trout
50ml double cream
100g Gruyère cheese, grated
sea salt and freshly ground black
  pepper

Bring a saucepan of salted water to the boil. Once boiling, drop in the asparagus spears and cook until tender and to the bite (about 3 minutes). Then refresh the asparagus in ice-cold water and drain on kitchen paper.

Cut the tips off the asparagus, place to one side for garnish, then finely slice the stems into thin rounds.

Crack the eggs into a large mixing bowl and whisk thoroughly. Add the chopped dill and the sliced asparagus stems and season.

Preheat the grill to its highest setting.

Warm a large ovenproof frying pan on the hob. Place the butter in the pan and when it starts to froth, pour in the egg mixture and gently move in the pan using a wooden spoon. When the egg just begins to set (about 2 minutes), remove from the heat – the egg mixture should still be fairly runny on the top at this point.

Carefully flake the smoked trout over the eggs, then add the asparagus tips. Drizzle over the cream, then top with the Gruyère cheese.

Place the pan near the top of the preheated grill and remove only when the cheese is golden and bubbling (about 1–2 minutes). The omelette should still be a little bit runny. Serve and enjoy.

Deep-fried Duck Eggs with Mushrooms and Parma Ham

All the girls in my house love their mushrooms – we go through so many! I make this for them at the weekend when I'm not under time constraints as I know they enjoy it so much and having a posh à-la-carte-style brekkie makes them feel special. It's called an investment, as for the rest of the day I can enjoy a cheeky beer or an afternoon's fishing!

serves **4**

4 duck eggs
75g plain flour
2 free-range hens' eggs
100g fresh Panko breadcrumbs
4 large field mushrooms, stalks
   removed
2 tablespoons olive oil
1 teaspoon fresh thyme leaves
vegetable oil, for frying
4 slices of Parma ham
sea salt and freshly ground black
   pepper

Preheat the oven to 180°C/ Gas mark 4.

Bring a pan of water to the boil. Gently lower the duck eggs into the pan and cook for 5 minutes, then remove with a slotted spoon and plunge into a bowl of cold water to refresh. Once cold, very carefully peel the eggs, place them on kitchen paper and gently pat dry.

Place the flour in one bowl, whisk the hens' eggs in a second bowl and place the breadcrumbs in a third bowl. Carefully roll the shelled duck eggs first in the flour, then in the egg mixture and lastly in breadcrumbs. Repeat this process again as this ensures the breadcrumbs stick.

Place the field mushrooms upside down (darkest side up) in a roasting tin, brush with olive oil, sprinkle over the thyme and season. Place in the oven and roast for 10–15 minutes until soft.

Plug in the deep-fat fryer (or place enough vegetable oil in a deep saucepan and heat to approximately 180°C). Using a slotted spoon or the fryer basket, gently place the breadcrumbed duck eggs into the oil and fry for 2–3 minutes until golden brown. Remove and place on kitchen paper to drain, then season.

Once the mushrooms are cooked, remove from the roasting tin and drain on kitchen paper.

Preheat the grill. Place the Parma ham on a roasting tray and grill until crispy on both sides.

Serve the duck eggs on top of the roasted mushrooms and topped with crispy Parma ham.

Pile-em-High Waffles, Crispy Smoked Bacon and Maple Syrup

There is something amazing when you combine salt and sweet flavours – they just work so well together. We love our trips to New York, and this dish is definitely on the cards at least once. The secret to success is to crisp up your pancetta or smoked streaky bacon really well.

serves **4**

250g plain flour
1 tablespoon baking powder
2 tablespoons caster sugar
1 teaspoon sea salt
2 free-range eggs
250ml buttermilk
200ml milk
2 tablespoons vegetable oil
spray oil, for waffle iron
16 slices of Pancetta or smoked streaky bacon
maple syrup, for drizzling

Sift the flour and baking powder into a bowl, then add the caster sugar and salt.

Separate the eggs. Place the whites into a clean bowl and whisk until you get soft peaks.

Add the yolks to the dry mix, then add the buttermilk, milk and finally 2 tablespoons of vegetable oil and whisk together to form a smooth batter (don't over-whisk or the mixture will become too heavy). Gently fold the egg whites into the batter.

Oil and heat the waffle iron and pour in the batter to the correct level. Cook until golden brown and cooked through, then repeat this process until you have run out of batter. If you wish, keep the waffles warm in a low oven.

Heat a large frying pan over a high heat, then add the pancetta or bacon and cook until crisp.

Pile up the waffles and crispy pancetta, then drizzle with maple syrup to your heart's content.

"There is something amazing when you combine salt and sweet flavours – they just work so well together."

The Family Kitchen

Cinnamon Toast and Orange Blossom Honey

This is one of Amber's favourites and when I want to get in her good books, I deliver this on a tray around 10am on a Sunday morning with a glass of freshly squeezed orange juice and the Sunday supplements.

serves **4**

3 large free-range eggs
125ml double cream
125ml semi-skimmed milk
1 teaspoon ground cinnamon
1 vanilla pod
zest of 1 large orange
1 large brioche loaf (300–400g)
3 tablespoons sunflower oil
50g butter
2 tablespoons orange blossom
   honey

Whisk together the eggs, cream, milk and cinnamon in a large bowl. Split the vanilla pod and use the back of the knife to scrape out all the seeds. Add these to the egg mixture, then thoroughly whisk in the orange zest.

Place a large frying pan over a medium heat, add the oil and butter and allow to melt.

Discard the ends from the brioche and cut the loaf into 8 slices around 2cm thick. Taking 2 slices of the brioche at a time, quickly dip into the egg mixture, letting any excess drain off. Place both slices in the pan and fry until golden brown (about 2 minutes), then turn over and fry for a further 2 minutes on the other side – both sides should be golden brown and crispy. Remove and drain on kitchen paper.

Repeat this process for the other slices. Once ready, pile up and drizzle generously with the lovely orange blossom honey.

Lazy Morning Smoked Salmon French Toast

This is a great take on smoked salmon and scrambled eggs. Julia Edmonds, a fellow colleague, gave me this recipe. It was so delicious that it had to have a place in this book. It works best with white bread for colour and flavour. Enjoy!

serves **4**

125ml double cream
125ml milk
3 free-range eggs
½ bunch of chives, finely chopped
50g cream cheese
8 medium-cut slices of white bread
200g smoked salmon, thinly sliced
2 tablespoons vegetable oil, for frying
20g butter, for frying
sea salt and freshly ground black pepper

Place the cream, milk, eggs and chives in a bowl. Season, whisk together and put to one side.

Spread the cream cheese over all 8 slices of bread, then layer the smoked salmon evenly on 4 of the slices. Top with the second slices, to make 4 sandwiches.

Heat a frying pan over a medium heat with a splash of the vegetable oil, then add a knob butter and allow to melt. Quickly dip each sandwich into the egg mixture, ensuring both sides are covered. Allow any excess mix to drain off, then fry until golden brown and crispy on one side, then turn over and fry the other side (about 3 minutes each side to cook through). Repeat for each sandwich.

Once cooked, drain and rest on kitchen paper for about 2 minutes, then season with black pepper. Serve cut into triangles.

The Family Kitchen

Marmalade and Honey-Glazed Ham with Fried Eggs

This ham is also great with The Ultimate Velvet Macaroni Cheese (see page 109) and my Balsamic-roasted Tomatoes (see page 70). If you've made some, try using the Seville Orange Marmalade (see page 155). I've used a large joint of meat which you'll get four really decent slices from.
If any is left over, it's great for sandwiches.

serves **4**

800g smoked gammon joint
250g marmalade
75g clear honey
1 tablespoon vegetable oil
4 free-range eggs
crusty bread, to serve

Place the gammon joint in a large saucepan and cover with water. Bring to the boil, then cover and simmer for 50–60 minutes (the temperature should reach 72ºC on a meat thermometer or probe by the end of the cooking time).

Remove the joint from the pan and allow to cool. Once cool, remove the skin with a sharp knife, leaving a layer of fat.

Preheat the oven to 180ºC/ Gas mark 4.

Tip the marmalade into a saucepan, and add the honey. Gently warm and stir together. Remove from the heat and allow to cool to room temperature.

Place the joint in a roasting tin, spoon over and brush on the marmalade and honey mixture. Place in the oven and roast for 20 minutes, frequently glazing with the sticky marmalade and honey mixture from the bottom of the roasting tin. Allow to rest for 10 minutes.

Heat the oil in a frying pan and shallow fry the eggs 'sunny side up'.

Carve the warm glazed ham and serve topped with a fried egg. Drizzle the pan juices over the top and mop up with a chunk of crusty bread.

The Family Kitchen

Kirby Club Sarnie

Everyone enjoys a good club sandwich and my take on it stacks up with the best of them. The sweetness of the mango and the saltiness of the smoked chicken are the stars of the show here. Hope you enjoy it as much as everyone in our house does!

serves **4**

16 slices of pancetta or bacon
2 breasts of smoked chicken, skinless
$\frac{1}{2}$ bunch of spring onions, chopped
$\frac{1}{4}$ bunch of coriander, roughly chopped
1 tablespoon mango chutney
4 tablespoons mayonnaise
$\frac{1}{2}$ iceberg lettuce, finely sliced
12 slices of farmhouse white bloomer, medium sliced
2 large dill pickles, thinly sliced lengthways into ribbons using a speed peeler
16 cherry tomatoes
8 skewers
sea salt and freshly ground black pepper

Preheat the oven to 160°C/ Gas mark 3. Line a baking tray with baking parchment.

Place the pancetta rashers on the lined baking tray and cover with another sheet of paper. Place a second baking tray on top of the paper – this will stop the pancetta from curling up and help to give it an extra-crispy finish. Cook the pancetta in the oven for 20 minutes until crisp, then take it out and allow it to cool to room temperature (leave the second baking tray on top while the pancetta cools).

Finely chop the chicken and place in a bowl with the spring onion, coriander, mango chutney and half the mayonnaise. Mix together, season and leave to one side.

Mix the lettuce and remaining mayonnaise together and season.

Toast the bread until golden brown.

To assemble, spoon the smoked chicken mix onto the first layer of toast, place a second slice of toast on top, then a layer of the lettuce and mayonnaise mix, top with 4 slices of crispy pancetta and a third slice of toast. Repeat to make another 3 sarnies.

Thread your ribbons of pickle around the tomatoes on each skewer and spike at opposite ends. Slice each sarnie through the middle and serve on a chopping board with a handful of crisps.

Jasper's Rack-it-up Slow-Cooked Maple 'n' Jack Daniels Ribs

There are very few weekends when Jasper hasn't asked for this. It's a fabulous dinner, it's big boys' portions and he says they're the best ribs ever! Well, that's pretty big hype but let's see what you think! Braising the ribs for a few hours in all those scrummy flavours really packs a punch. This is heads-down stuff and surrender to the stickiness!

serves 4

1.5kg pork spare ribs
2 onions, sliced
4 bay leaves
1 cinnamon stick
2 star anise
2 garlic cloves, crushed
750ml chicken stock
750ml apple juice

For the smoky sauce
6 tablespoons maple syrup
125ml Jack Daniels
2 tablespoons muscovado sugar
1 tablespoon Worcestershire
  sauce
1 red chilli, deseeded and finely
  chopped
juice of 2 limes
$1/2$ bottle of HP Sauce

Preheat the oven to 160°C/Gas mark 3.

Place the pork ribs, onions, bay leaves, cinnamon stick, star anise and garlic in a roasting tin measuring about 35 x 30 x 5cm. Pour over the stock and apple juice, making sure to cover the ribs. Cover with kitchen foil and braise the ribs slowly in the oven for 3 hours.

Remove the roasting tin from the oven and carefully pour and strain off all the stock into a large saucepan (there should be about 500–750ml remaining). Leave the ribs in the roasting tray and place to one side. Leave the oven on.

Whisk into the stock the maple syrup, Jack Daniels, sugar, Worcestershire sauce, red chilli, lime juice and HP Sauce. Bring up to a rapid boil and reduce down to around half (this will take around 15 minutes).

Pour the sticky glaze onto the braised ribs, ensuring they are completely covered.

Increase the oven temperature to 190°C/Gas mark 5. Place the ribs back in the hot oven for about 15–20 minutes, to colour, crisp and caramelise.

The Family Kitchen

Nifty Nachos

How easy is this? This is a great recipe to have to hand if you end up with a room full of teenagers who somehow seem to have claimed residence in the lounge and show no sign of going home! Throw in a few DVDs and bottles of Coke, then close the door! Meanwhile, you and your beloved share a nice glass of wine together and stay well clear of the noise! For a great alternative, you could use smoked chicken or maybe a smoked cheese.

serves **4–6**

200g tortilla chips
200g jar of sliced jalapeños, drained
200g mature Cheddar cheese, grated
200ml soured cream
2 limes, quartered

For the salsa
200g cooked chicken breast, cut into 1cm cubes
4 plum tomatoes, deseeded and diced
1 bunch of spring onions, finely shredded
1 ripe avocado, peeled, stoned and cubed
$1/2$ bunch of coriander
1 red chilli, deseeded and finely chopped
1 teaspoon olive oil
sea salt and freshly ground black pepper

Preheat the oven to 180°C/ Gas mark 4.

Place the chicken, tomatoes, spring onions and avocado in a large bowl. Chop half of the coriander and add to the bowl with the chilli and olive oil. Gently fold all the salsa ingredients together, then season.

Scatter a third of the tortilla chips over the base of a large ovenproof dish, then smother with half the salsa mix, half the jalapeños and half the grated cheese. Add another layer of tortilla chips, the rest of the salsa mix and jalapeños. Add the final layer of tortilla chips and top with the remaining cheese.

Place in the hot oven and cook until cheese is caramelised and gooey, about 8–10 minutes. Remove from oven and generously dollop with soured cream and garnish with the remaining coriander and the limes.

Creamy Garlic Mussels
with Skinny Rosemary Fries

serves **4**

Creamy garlic mussels

Saturday night, you've got a great movie picked so what could be better than some succulent sweet mussels in a lovely garlicky creamy broth, some amazing fries and a quality beer to wash it all down. Get stuck in and get messy.

1.5kg mussels
2 tablespoons vegetable oil
2 onions, finely chopped
1 leek, chopped into 1cm rounds
3 garlic cloves, chopped and crushed
1 star anise
175ml dry vermouth
300ml double cream
½ bunch of flat-leaf parsley, roughly chopped
25g Parmesan cheese, finely grated
sea salt and freshly ground black pepper

Tip the mussels into a colander and rinse under cold running water. Remove any beards attached to the mussels and discard any open mussels or those with broken shells.

Place a large lidded saucepan over a high heat, add the oil and allow to smoke. Quickly add the onions, leek, garlic, star anise, mussels and the vermouth. Place a tight-fitting lid on top and gently shake the pan over a high heat for around 4–5 minutes. Remove from the heat – when cooked, all the mussels should be open wide (discard any that have not opened).

Using a slotted spoon, transfer the mussels into a bowl ready for serving, leaving the leeks and onions in the stock.

Place the saucepan back onto the heat, bring to the boil and reduce for 2 minutes. Stir in the double cream, bring back to the boil to reduce (about 7 minutes), then season. Pour the cream sauce over the mussels and finish with the parsley and Parmesan.

Skinny rosemary fries

These fries really are great. The crispy garlic shavings and deep-fried rosemary with the rock-salt mix are a nod to the Spotted Pig in New York. You can make your own fries, but I've used shop-bought skinny ones for ease. Make sure you slice the garlic very thinly, like flaked almonds.

700g skinny chips (shop-bought)
2 tablespoons olive oil
½ bunch of rosemary, leaves picked (around 70 single leaves)
4 garlic cloves, thinly sliced
2 tablespoons good-quality rock salt

Preheat the oven to 200°C/ Gas mark 6.

Place the chips on a baking tray in the oven and cook for 20 minutes until brown and crispy.

Pour the olive oil into a frying pan and heat over a medium heat. Add the rosemary leaves and sliced garlic and gently fry, stirring continually, for around 3 minutes until golden brown and crispy. Drain on kitchen paper.

Place the rock salt into a small bowl and add the fried rosemary and garlic – this is now your seasoning. Shake the seasoning over your fries. Serve in individual bowls next to your creamy mountain of mussels.

Big Weekend Chill

Tempura Crispy Vegetables & Soy Dipping Sauce

This is a fantastic starter or snack on a Saturday night and it's great served with some garlic mayo, soy sauce or sweet chilli dipping sauce – whatever takes your fancy! This is a first-rate tempura batter recipe. The Japanese don't overwork the batter, leaving a few small lumps. In fact, they use their chopsticks to mix it. When cooked, this keeps the batter light and airy.

serves **4**

vegetable oil, for frying
1 red pepper, de-seeded and cut lengthways into strips around 1cm thick
1 courgette, sliced diagonally, about 1cm thick
1 small aubergine, halved lengthways and sliced, about 1cm thick
1 red onion, sliced into onion rings, about 1cm thick
1 large flat mushroom, sliced 1cm thick
2 limes, quartered
soy sauce, for dipping
sea salt and freshly ground black pepper

For the tempura batter
200g self-raising flour
100g cornflour
450ml ice-cold sparkling water

To make the batter, sift the self-raising flour and cornflour into a large mixing bowl. Gradually stir in the ice-cold sparkling water until a batter consistency is reached which easily coats your finger. Don't overwork the batter – some lumps are fine!

Plug in the deep-fat fryer or place enough vegetable oil in a deep saucepan and heat to approximately 180ºC.

Coat the vegetables in tempura batter, then gently drop each piece individually into the fryer. Fry in small batches as this stops them from sticking together. Cook to a light golden brown and crispy, around 2 minutes.

Drain on kitchen paper. Season and serve in bamboo baskets with fresh lime and soy sauce.

"A fantastic starter or snack on a Saturday night."

The Family Kitchen

Crispy Potato and Smoked Paprika Wedges with Fresh Chilli and Lime Mayonnaise

We love picky bits in our house. Saturday night is movie night, so the iPads and Blackberrys are put away for the evening and we all squeeze on the sofa together. These wedges are perfect for that kind of evening, when you don't want too much but just nice picky food. However, if you fancy more, this is great cuddled up next to a bucket of Kirby Fried Buttermilk Chicken (see page 89). Dip in!

serves **4**

2 large baking potatoes
1 large sweet potato
4 tablespoons vegetable oil
1 teaspoon smoked paprika
1 teaspoon sea salt
1 red chilli, de-seeded and finely chopped
juice of 1 lime
8 tablespoons mayonnaise

Preheat the oven to 180°C/ Gas mark 4. Line a baking tray with baking parchment.

Cut the potato and sweet potato into wedges, wash in cold water and pat dry with kitchen paper. Rub the wedges with the oil, then dust with the smoked paprika and sea salt and place on the baking tray. Roast in the oven for 30 minutes, turning over after 15 minutes to colour nicely on each side. This should leave them crispy on the outside and soft and fluffy on the inside.

Meanwhile, mix together the fresh chilli, lime juice and mayonnaise; keep to one side to serve with the wedges.

Once the wedges are cooked, place them on kitchen paper to drain and serve.

Saturday's X-Factor Open Steak Sandwich

Oooh, this will have the family drooling! The headliner in this dish is the butter. In my days of working in hotels, it was very trendy to make your own house butters, the most famous being that of the Café de Paris. This is the 'Kirby House' butter and it will liven up any grilled fish or meat. It's also totally sublime melted over Jersey Royal potatoes.

serves 4

vegetable oil, for deep-fat frying
4 x 125g good-quality rib-eye
    steak
3 tablespoons olive oil
2 x 15–20cm ciabatta, split
    lengthways
1 red onion, finely sliced into rings
1 bunch or packet of watercress
sea salt and freshly ground black
    pepper

For the X-Factor butter
250g butter, at room temperature
1 tablespoon balsamic vinegar
2 teaspoons horseradish sauce
1 teaspoon each of cayenne
    pepper, rock salt, smoked
    paprika, garlic powder and
    English mustard powder
$1/4$ bunch of fresh tarragon,
    chopped

For the tempura batter
100g self-raising flour
50g cornflour
225ml ice-cold sparkling water

Place the butter in a mixing bowl and gently stir in all the other ingredients, ensuring they are thoroughly mixed together. Spoon the butter in a line along the edge of a sheet of baking parchment, roll into a rolling pin shape, then twist each end to make a cracker shape. Chill in the fridge for 1 hour. (This will store happily in the fridge for up to 1 month – you won't need to use it all for this recipe.)

To make the tempura batter, sift the self-raising flour and cornflour into a large mixing bowl. Gradually stir in the ice-cold sparkling water until a batter consistency is reached which should easily coat your finger. Don't over-work the batter – some lumps are fine!

Plug in your deep-fat fryer, or place enough vegetable oil in a deep saucepan, and heat to approximately 180°C.

Place a ridged grill pan over the heat until hot and smoking. Rub the rib-eye steaks in oil and seasoning, and chargrill to your liking (medium rare is best – 3 minutes on each side), then take off the griddle and allow to rest.

Place the ciabatta halves straight on to the griddle pan, allowing the bread to soak up all the meaty juices and lightly colour on both sides.

Dip the onion rings and watercress in the tempura batter to coat lightly, then carefully lower into the hot oil. Do this individually so that they don't stick together. Cook for 2 minutes until crisp, remove from the oil using a slotted spoon and drain on a plate lined with kitchen paper and season.

To assemble, remove the butter from the baking parchment and, using a hot knife, cut into slices 5mm thick. Slice the steaks in half lengthways and place on the toasted ciabatta. Top with the butter slices and pile on the tempura watercress and onions. Serve on a chopping board with a steak knife.

The Family Kitchen

Fat Garam Masala Chips with Spicy Mango Mayo

Even though I think chips with curry sauce is a culinary abomination, it seems I am alone in this! I give in gracefully and have put my own slant on this with a nice mango mayo, but if you insist on a curry sauce, the Katsu Curry Sauce (see page 95) is perfect with these chips (although my family will actually go to the Chinese takeaway and just order a tub of curry sauce!).

serves 4

5 very large potatoes, such as
   Maris Piper
vegetable oil, for frying
$1/2$ teaspoon Homemade Garam
   Masala (see page 51), or
   shop bought
1 teaspoon ground sea salt

Peel the potatoes and cut into chips, about 8–10cm in length, 2cm wide and 2cm thick. This will give you a perfect 'fat chip'! Rinse in a colander under cold running water and pat dry with kitchen paper.

Plug in the deep-fat fryer or place enough vegetable oil in a deep saucepan and heat to approximately 160°C. Lower the chips into the oil and blanch slowly for around 8–10 minutes (this means cook without colouring). Lift out the chip basket or use a slotted spoon to remove the chips gently from the pan.

Turn the heat up to 180°C, allow the oil to get up to temperature, then return the chips to the fryer and cook until golden brown and crispy (about 2–3 minutes).

Drain in a colander and then on kitchen paper. Mix the garam masala and sea salt together, then generously dust the chips. Serve piled high, ready for dunking into the curry mango mayo.

Mango Mayo

enough to serve 4

8 tablespoons mayonnaise
1 tablespoon Homemade Curry
   Powder (see page 51)
1 tablespoon smooth mango
   chutney
$1/4$ bunch of coriander, chopped
sea salt and freshly ground black
   pepper

Spoon the mayonnaise into a bowl, then whisk in the curry powder and then stir in the mango chutney. Fold in the chopped coriander and season.

Kirby Fried Buttermilk Chicken

The buttermilk makes the difference here, as it seems to tenderise the chicken and make it more succulent. When you double dip the coating mix, it makes the coating extra crispy. This chicken will give the good ol' colonel a run for his money!

serves **4**

4 chicken breasts, cut into strips
2 free-range eggs
72g plain flour
200g fresh panko breadcrumbs
125ml sunflower oil
sea salt and freshly ground black
  pepper

For the marinade
285ml cultured buttermilk
2 garlic cloves, finely chopped
1 small onion, finely chopped
2 teaspoons clear honey

Mix all marinade ingredients together in a bowl. Add the chicken, making sure it is well covered, then cover the bowl with clingfilm and leave in the fridge to marinate overnight.

When ready to cook the chicken, drain and reserve the marinade. Pat the chicken breasts dry with kitchen paper.

Whisk the eggs into the remaining marinade, then keep to one side. Put the flour and breadcrumbs in 2 separate bowls. You should now have 3 separate bowls in front of you. Dip the chicken into the flour, then into the buttermilk marinade and finally into the breadcrumbs. Do this twice – you'll end up with a really crispy coating when you fry the chicken.

Heat the sunflower oil in a shallow pan over a medium heat, then drop the chicken in and fry until the breadcrumbs are golden brown. You'll know when the oil is hot enough as it will sizzle when you drop a bit of breadcrumb in. Don't overload the pan with too much chicken and fry in batches to stop them from sticking together.

Once cooked, place on kitchen paper and pat to remove any excess oil before serving.

"This chicken will give the good ol colonel a run for his money!"

N.Y.C. Short Rib Sliders

We've made these for the kids, who adore them, and as canapés for adults, who equally love them. It's so easy to make your own burgers and what's even better is you know exactly what's going in them!

serves **4**

(makes 12 little burgers)

300g boneless short rib beef, minced
$^1/_2$ onion, finely diced
1 free-range egg
1 tablespoon HP Sauce
splash of Worcestershire sauce
60g Roquefort cheese, cut into 12 pieces
12 mini seeded burger buns, or mini brioche buns if you prefer
60g rocket leaves
6 cherry tomatoes, sliced
12 wooden skewers
sea salt and freshly ground black pepper

In a large bowl, combine the mince, onion, egg, HP Sauce, Worcestershire sauce and seasoning. Once the mixture has come together, divide and roll it into 12 little balls (about the size of a golf ball), then flatten each ball into a burger shape.

Preheat the grill to a high setting. Grill the burgers for 5 minutes, until they are cooked through and any fat that comes out is clear. Don't forget to flip them over while they are grilling, to colour both sides evenly. Once the burgers are cooked through, remove them briefly from the grill. Place a piece of Roquefort on each, then return them to the grill until the cheese melts. While the cheese is melting, toast the buns so that they are ready for the burgers.

Once the cheese has melted, remove the burgers from the grill and pop them into the buns, adding a small amount of rocket and two slices of tomato to each. Spear them with a wooden skewer and serve.

The Family Kitchen

Funky Fish 'n' Chips

Fish and chips with a twist! **Salmon is an excellent super food and the caraway seeds in the batter are amazing. Cook this for a change and blow the family away with your culinary expertise! Try my Fat Garam Masala Chips (see page 88) with this fish as their spices complement each other perfectly.**

serves **4**

600g salmon fillet, skinned
6 large floury potatoes
vegetable oil, for frying
1 tablespoon plain flour, for
    dusting
2 lemons, halved
sea salt and freshly ground black
    pepper

For the caraway batter
80g plain flour
60g cornflour
1 teaspoon baking powder
100ml lager
50ml sparkling water
juice of $1/2$ lemon
1 teaspoons caraway seeds
$1/4$ teaspoon tumeric
1 teaspoon rock salt

To make the batter, sift the plain flour, cornflour and baking powder into a large mixing bowl. Whisk in the lager, sparkling water and lemon juice, then add the caraway seeds, turmeric and rock salt. Whisk to make a light and airy batter – this should have the consistency of double cream and coat the back of a spoon. Cover and place to one side.

Cut the salmon fillet into strips around 6cm in length and 2cm wide, and place in a bowl.

Peel the potatoes and cut into chips about 8cm in length, 1cm wide and 1cm thick. Rinse in a colander and pat dry with kitchen paper.

Plug in the deep-fat fryer or place enough vegetable oil in a deep saucepan and heat to approximately 160°C. Lower the chips into the oil and blanch slowly for around 5 minutes (this means cook without colouring). Lift out the chip basket or use a slotted spoon to remove the chips gently from the pan. Turn the heat up to 180°C, allow the oil to get up to temperature, then return the chips to the fryer and continue frying until golden brown and crispy (about 2–3 minutes). Drain on kitchen paper and season.

Gently dust each salmon strip with flour, then dip into the batter, ensuring they are well covered. Carefully lower into the fryer and cook at 170°C until golden brown, around 3–5 minutes. Remove and drain on kitchen paper.

Serve in a newspaper cone lined with baking parchment and with lemon halves.

The Family Kitchen

Jammin' Sweet Potato with Rice and Peas

Every year, Amber and I let ourselves loose on Notting Hill Carnival. The aroma and taste of this dish take us straight back there. Cue the reggae and a can of Red Stripe!

serves **4**

2 large orange-flesh sweet
  potatoes
50ml vegetable oil
1 teaspoon rock salt
1 onion, finely sliced
75g long-grain rice
100ml coconut milk
100g tin of kidney beans, drained
1 teaspoon fresh thyme, chopped
1 whole red chilli
smoked Tabasco chipotle sauce,
  to taste
100ml crème fraîche
1/2 bunch of spring onions,
  chopped
sea salt and freshly ground black
  pepper

Preheat the oven to 180°C/
Gas mark 4.

Cut the sweet potatoes in half lengthways, then place in a bowl with half the vegetable oil and the rock salt. Roll the potatoes until they are completely covered in oil and salt, then place on a baking tray and bake in the oven for about 1 hour until cooked through.

Heat the remaining oil in a large saucepan and fry the onion without colouring for 3 minutes. Add the rice to the pan and stir together, then pour in 100ml water and bring to the boil.

Add in the coconut milk, kidney beans, fresh thyme and chilli, cover and simmer for around 20 minutes, stirring occasionally, until the rice is tender. Remove the whole chilli and discard, season to taste and place to one side to keep warm.

Remove the sweet potatoes from the oven. Carefully spoon out the flesh, place in a bowl and roughly mash with a fork. Add in the rice and peas and fold very gently together, then spoon back into the sweet potato skins. Season with chipotle sauce and spoon over the crème fraîche. Top with chopped spring onions.

"Every year, Amber and I let ourselves loose on Notting Hill Carnival. The aroma and taste of this dish take us straight back there."

Big Weekend Chill

Chicken Katsu, Jasmine Rice and Pickled Cucumber Salad

This is very tasty and it's one of our kids' favourite dinners. It's well worth the effort and completely knocks the socks off the ready-to-make kits you can buy in the supermarkets.

serves **4**

For the marinade
400ml coconut milk
2 garlic cloves, finely chopped
3 teaspoons clear honey
$1/2$ teaspoon cracked black pepper
$1/2$ teaspoon sea salt
zest and juice of 1 lime

For the chicken
4 chicken breasts, cut into strips
    8 x 2cm
2 free-range eggs
100g plain flour
200g Panko (Japanese
    breadcrumbs)
125ml sunflower oil
sea salt and freshly ground black
    pepper

For the sauce
3 tablespoons vegetable oil
1 white onion, chopped
2 cloves of garlic, chopped
5cm piece of root ginger, peeled
    and grated
1 large red chilli, deseeded and
    finely chopped
2 tablespoons plain flour
1 tablespoon mild Curry Powder
    (see page 51)
1 tablespoon Garam Marsala (see
    page 51)
1 teaspoon smoked paprika

300ml chicken stock
1 tablespoon honey
1 tablespoon mango chutney
1 tablespoon soy sauce

For the rice
280g jasmine rice, washed

For the pickled cucumber salad
1 cucumber, peeled lengthways
    to make ribbons
1 tablespoon rice wine vinegar
$1/2$ teaspoon sugar
$1/2$ red chilli, chopped

Combine all the ingredients for the marinade in a large bowl. Add the chicken and stir to coat completely, then cover with cling-film and refrigerate overnight.

Next day, remove the chicken from the marinade and pat dry with kitchen paper.

Add the eggs to the remaining marinade and whisk together. Sift the flour into a bowl and place the breadcrumbs into a separate bowl. You should now have 3 bowls in front of you. Dip the chicken strips first into the flour, then in the marinade and egg mix and finally into the breadcrumbs, making sure they are coated on all sides, then dip again in the marinade and egg mix, then the breadcrumbs for a really crispy coating.

To make the sauce, heat the oil in a saucepan, add the chopped onion, garlic, ginger and chilli and

gently fry until soft. Stir in the flour, curry powder, garam masala and paprika to form a paste. Slowly add the chicken stock until it thickens and cook slowly for a further 10 minutes. Stir in the honey, mango chutney and soy sauce to taste, place to one side and keep warm.

Bring a large pan of salted water to the boil. Stir in the rice, return to the boil, cover and simmer for 10 minutes. Drain well and leave to stand.

To make the pickled cucumber salad, place the cucumber ribbons in a bowl with rice wine vinegar, sugar and chopped chilli and leave to pickle while you cook the chicken.

Heat the sunflower oil in a shallow pan over a medium heat, then drop the chicken in and fry until the breadcrumbs are golden brown. You'll know when the oil is hot enough as it will sizzle when you drop a few breadcrumbs in. Don't overload the pan with too much chicken – you may need to cook it in batches.

Once the chicken is cooked, dab with kitchen paper to remove any excess oil and season before serving. Bring all the elements together on the table and serve however you like!

Real Sesame Prawn Toast

Another 'must' for the family's cosy night in with everyone sprawled on the sofa in front of the box. Dish these out and regain the power over the remote control! For a bit of fun and authenticity, we serve these in takeaway containers.

serves **4**

250g raw king or tiger prawns, peeled
2 free-range egg whites
1 tablespoon fish sauce
1 tablespoon soy sauce
30g cornflour
5 tablespoons sesame seeds
6 slices of medium-cut white bread
6 tablespoons sweet chilli dipping sauce
sea salt and freshly ground black pepper

Place the peeled raw prawns into a blender and blitz thoroughly for around 2 minutes. Pour the egg whites in while blitzing, add the fish sauce and soy sauce and finally the cornflour, blend completely for about 1 minute.

Spread the mixture evenly across the slices of bread, cover with sesame seeds and pat down gently with a palette knife.

Plug in the deep-fat fryer or place enough vegetable oil in a deep saucepan and heat to approximately 180°C. Place in a square of toast and cook one at a time, turning gently with a spoon until crispy brown (about 3–4 minutes).

Drain on kitchen paper and season. Cut into triangles and serve stacked in a noodle box with the sweet chilli sauce on the side.

"Another must for the family's cosy night in with everyone sprawled on the sofa in front of the box."

The Family Kitchen

Funk-it-up Fajitas

There are many recipes for fajitas. This one is a little more involved but well worth the effort! The chorizo really warms this up and the pomegranate gives it lovely texture and bite. Slap on the guacamole and get amongst it!

serves **4**

For the dry rub
1 tablespoon each of brown sugar, garlic powder, smoked paprika, cayenne pepper, mild chilli powder, ground cumin and rock salt

For the guacamole
2 ripe Hass avocados, peeled and stoned (retain the stones)
1 green chilli, finely chopped
$1/4$ bunch of coriander
juice of 1 lime
freshly ground black pepper

For the filling
3 x 150g chicken breasts, sliced into strips
150g mini chorizo, sliced in half lengthways (or 2 normal sized, sliced)
1 red onion, sliced
2 peppers, sliced
1 whole pomegranate, seeded
2 whole plum tomatoes, chopped
$1/4$ bunch of coriander, roughly chopped

3 tablespoons vegetable oil
8 flour tortillas
120g strong Cheddar cheese, grated
200ml crème fraîche

Place all dry rub ingredients in a bag and shake to mix. Store in an airtight container (this will keep for a couple of months).

Rub 2 tablespoons of your dry mix with 1 tablespoon vegetable oil to make a paste, then rub the paste into the sliced chicken. Cover and leave in the fridge to marinate for at least 2 hours.

To make the guacamole, place the avocado in a mortar and smash with the pestle until chunky. Fold in the chopped chilli, coriander and lime juice. Season to taste with ground black pepper. Place in a bowl with one of the avocado stones in the middle (this stops the guacamole from going brown), cover with clingfilm and keep in the fridge.

Preheat the oven to 150°C/ Gas mark 2.

Place a frying pan or wok over a high heat, add 1 tablespoon of vegetable oil and heat until smoking. Sear the marinated chicken and chorizo for 5 minutes or until cooked and tender, remove from the heat and drain in a colander.

Using the same pan, add the remaining vegetable oil and cook the onions and peppers until tender. Add the drained chicken and chorizo, chopped tomatoes and pomegranate seeds. Season to taste, then place in a funky serving dish. Stir in the coriander. Warm the flour tortillas in the oven for a few minutes. Place the crème fraîche, guacamole and grated cheese in separate bowls. Place all the ingredients in the middle of the table and get stuck in.

Big Weekend Chill

Whole-Roasted Brie, Roasted Jersey Royals and Crispy Pancetta

Use a good-quality Brie or Camembert, but remember to buy one that is boxed as this supports the cheese while it is roasting in the oven. We serve this when we have a few friends over for drinks and it disappears so quickly! The great thing is it doesn't take too much effort and it's a crowd pleaser! Cheese doesn't last long in our house and this is my lovely Tabitha's favourite for a spoily treat.

serves **4**

300g Jersey Royal baby new
  potatoes, or similar
8 slices pancetta
1 leek, sliced into 5mm rounds
2 garlic cloves, sliced into very
  thin slivers
5 tablespoons olive oil
1 whole Brie (500g), in a box
1 tablespoon clear honey
1 teaspoon sea salt
rock salt and freshly ground black
  pepper for seasoning

Preheat the oven to 170°C/
Gas mark 3½.

Place the new potatoes in a saucepan and cover with salted water. Parboil over a medium heat until they are three-quarters cooked, then drain in a colander and tip into a roasting tin. Keep to one side.

Line a baking tray with baking parchment and place the pancetta rashers on top of this. Cover the rashers with another sheet of paper and place a second baking tray on top of the paper – this will stop the bacon from curling and help to give it an extra-crisp finish. Cook in the oven for 20 minutes until it is crisp.

Add the leeks and garlic to the roasting tin of new potatoes. Add 4 tablespoons of olive oil, rock salt and black pepper and place in the oven for 15–20 minutes, shaking and stirring occasionally until crisp and soft. Remove from the oven and keep warm.

Remove the Brie from its box and discard any paper wrappings. Soak the box in water for 5 minutes (this prevents it from splitting in the oven).

Place the Brie back into its box and place the base of the box inside the lid for support and then drizzle with remaining olive oil and the honey, then roast for about 7–10 minutes until gooey and soft.

Serve on a chopping block with the Brie in its box and the crispy new potatoes and leeks alongside, topped with crispy pancetta piled on top.

The Family Kitchen

Crispy Roasties and Aioli

Potatoes are always a big hit in our house! These are great set in the middle of the table with plenty of aioli to dip into. Smoked garlic also works well in the aioli for a change. Our local pub landlady, Kim at The Pier Hotel, puts these delicious roasties out and keeps us in!

serves **4**

1kg potatoes (I like to use Maris Piper), peeled and quartered
1 tablespoon plain flour, for dusting
6 tablespoons olive oil
1 tablespoon sea salt, for seasoning
2 sprigs of rosemary leaves, picked and roughly chopped

For the aioli
4 free-range egg yolks
6 garlic cloves, chopped and crushed
$\frac{1}{2}$ teaspoon English mustard
200ml olive oil
100ml sunflower oil
juice of $\frac{1}{2}$ lemon
sea salt and freshly ground black pepper

Preheat the oven to 190°C/ Gas mark 5.

Wash the potatoes under cold running water to remove any starch, then place in a large saucepan and cover with water, season and bring to the boil. Cook for about 8–10 minutes until parboiled. Drain thoroughly in a colander, then dust with flour and shake to fluff up the outside edges (this makes them crispy when cooked).

Pour the oil into a large roasting tray and heat in the oven for about 3 minutes until the oil is smoking.

Using a large spoon, very carefully add the potatoes to the roasting tray and ensure they are covered in the hot oil. Season well with sea salt, turning the potatoes carefully with a spoon. Place back in the oven for 30–40 minutes, mixing in the rosemary leaves halfway through cooking and occasionally shaking the pan and turning the potatoes until they are crispy, golden and delicious.

Remove and place on kitchen paper to drain.

While the potatoes are roasting, make the aioli. In a mixing bowl, combine the egg yolks, garlic and English mustard, then slowly whisk in both oils, ensuring they emulsify (as if you were making mayonnaise). Finally add the lemon juice and season. If the aioli is a little thick, add a splash of warm water. Serve next to the crispy roasties, ready for dunking – a perfect brunch!

Crackling Pig Sticks with Bramley Apple and Sage Sauce

You won't be able to keep your trotters off these tasty bites! They are great teamed with a nice beer and the Sunday papers. The homemade apple sauce is amazing – it's well worth doubling up the recipe and keeping some in the freezer for the next time you cook roast pork.

serves **4**,

makes **10-12** *strips*

300g pork skin (the rind from the loin, around 30cm in length and 16cm wide)
$\frac{1}{2}$ teaspoon table salt
1 teaspoon sea salt
1 teaspoon chopped fresh thyme

Trim the pork rind so you have a thin, even covering, around 1cm, of fat on the underside.

Season the fat side (non-skin side) of the rind with $\frac{1}{2}$ teaspoon of table salt. Roll the rind up from one of the short sides, then wrap in clingfilm as tightly as possible and tie both ends to prevent it from unrolling. Place in the freezer for 2 hours. The rind should be frozen but not solid – if it is, leave it to defrost just enough that you can cut through it.

Preheat the oven to 190°C/ Gas mark 5. Line a baking tray with baking parchment.

Mix the sea salt and thyme together in a bowl.

Using a sharp serrated knife, cut the rind into slices 5mm thick. Carefully unroll each one and place skin side up on the lined baking tray, leaving a 1cm gap between each slice. Once you have all the slices on the tray, season them with the sea salt and thyme and place a second sheet of baking parchment on top, followed by a second baking tray. You will then need to place something heavy and ovenproof on top of the baking tray to hold it down (I use a cast-iron casserole dish).

Place in the preheated oven and cook for 30 minutes, checking occasionally. The pig sticks are ready when golden brown. Remove from the oven, leave to cool for 5 minutes, then drain on kitchen paper. As they cool, they will crisp up more, but they can be eaten warm or cold.

Apple and Sage Sauce

4 large cooking apples (Bramleys are ideal), peeled and cored
50g butter
4 tablespoons caster sugar
3 tablespoons cider
1 teaspoon chopped fresh sage leaves

Cut the apples into 5mm cubes. Place the butter in a frying pan over a medium heat. When the butter begins to froth, add the apples, sugar, cider and sage. Cook gently for around 15 minutes or until the apple just starts to soften. Pour into a dish for dipping and serve warm.

The Family Kitchen

Sticky Toffee Date and Chicken Tatin

Use four mini blini pans (mini frying pans) or tart cases for this recipe, which is a savoury version of the classic French apple Tarte Tatin. I have made this countless times and it's a really impressive lunch dish. A great variation is to use salmon and fennel, and for the vegetarians amongst us try red onion, thyme and goat's cheese – all truly spectacular and all three have helped me win various chef competitions.

serves **4**

30g butter, for greasing
2 tablespoons olive oil
4 x 125g corn-fed chicken
  breasts, skin on, bone off
1 tablespoon flour, for dusting
30g butter
100g caster sugar
250g puff pastry
4 Medjool toffee dates
1 teaspoon fresh thyme leaves
rock salt and freshly ground black
  pepper

Generously butter 4 mini blini pans, mini frying pans or tart cases, then line the bottoms with a circle of baking parchment – this will enable the tarts to be turned out easily later on.

Place a large frying pan over a medium-high heat and add the olive oil. Season the chicken with rock salt and black pepper, then carefully place the chicken into the pan skin side down. Fry for around 2–3 minutes until the skin is golden brown, then turn and cook for a further 2–3 minutes on the other side. Remove from the pan and leave to cool. Gently melt the butter in a small saucepan over a low heat. Once butter has melted, add the sugar and 30ml water, and stir until it has combined, then increase the heat slightly. Cook and stir the mixture until it starts to caramelise and turn a lovely golden brown. While still hot, very carefully divide the caramel mixture evenly between the 4 buttered pans and place to one side for the caramel to go hard.

Lightly flour a work surface and roll out the puff pastry to a thickness of about 5mm. Cut out 4 circles of pastry using a side plate that has a diameter 2cm larger than the caramel pans. Leave the pastry to rest in the fridge for 10 minutes.

Preheat the oven to 190°C/ Gas mark 5.

Cut the dates in half and remove the stones. Arrange 2 date halves in each pan along with $1/4$ teaspoon of fresh thyme. Place a chicken breast in each pan, skin side down (if the chicken does not fit perfectly into the pan, you may need to trim slightly).

Remove the pastry circles from the fridge and place one on top of each chicken. Carefully tuck the pastry down around the chicken and the inside of the pan to create a good seal, ensuring you keep to the shape of the pan. Make a small hole in the top of the pastry to let the steam escape.

Place the pans on a baking tray and into the preheated oven. Bake for 12–15 minutes until the pastry is golden brown and the caramel is bubbling round the outside. If you have a meat thermometer or probe, the chicken should reach 65–70°C. Remove from the oven and leave to cool for 30 seconds.

To turn out, swiftly and carefully turn the pans over to allow the chicken tatins to drop out onto 4 plates. Make sure you do this while they are still warm as this will stop them from sticking. Remove the parchment or baking parchment and serve.

Field Mushroom Penne Pasta with Garlic Dough Balls

Completely moreish – I guarantee you will not have any of this left! Serve it in the middle of the table so everyone can dig in and help themselves, family style.

serves **4**

400g penne pasta
3 tablespoons olive oil
1 leek, sliced into 1cm rounds
1 large onion, finely chopped
3 cloves of garlic, peeled and crushed
300g mixed mushrooms, sliced 1cm thick
200ml white wine (optional)
1 vegetable stock cube
1 tablespoon wholegrain mustard
568ml double cream
$\frac{1}{2}$ bunch basil leaves, torn
50g Parmesan cheese, grated
1 tablespoon good-quality olive oil, for finishing
sea salt and freshly ground black pepper
Garlic Dough Balls, to serve (see page 107)

Fill a large saucepan with salted water and bring to the boil. Add the pasta and stir, then bring to a rolling boil for 11–13 minutes until tender and cooked al dente. Remove, place in a colander and refresh under cold running water. Drain the pasta thoroughly, then pat dry with kitchen paper.

Place a large saucepan over a medium heat, add 2 tablespoons of the oil and heat, then add the leeks, onion and garlic and cook without colouring for about 5 minutes. Turn up the heat, then add another tablespoon of olive oil, add the mushrooms and fry for a further 8–10 minutes, until cooked through.

Add the white wine (or water, if you prefer), stock cube (making sure it dissolves) and mustard and stir thoroughly into the mushrooms and onions. Reduce for 3–5 minutes, continually stirring to ensure it doesn't stick. Finally, pour in the double cream, bring to the boil and reduce down by a third (around 8–10 minutes), stirring occasionally. Gently tip in the cooked pasta, season and stir together for a further 2 minutes, making sure it's hot for serving.

Place in a big pasta bowl and add the torn basil leaves, Parmesan and a glug of olive oil. Serve with freshly ground black pepper and Garlic Dough Balls.

"Serve it in the middle of the table so everyone can dig in and help themselves, family style."

The Family Kitchen

Garlic dough balls

These are 'totes amazeballs', to quote the family! Very garlicky and great for mopping up the sauce from Field Mushroom Penne Pasta (see page 106). Try adding dried chilli to the dough to spice it up a bit if the fancy takes you.

serves **4**

15g fresh yeast or 1 x 7g packet
140ml warm water
250g strong white flour, sifted
$\frac{1}{2}$ teaspoon caster sugar
pinch of sea salt
2 garlic cloves, finely chopped
2 tablespoons finely chopped
   chives

For the garlic butter
125g very soft butter
1 teaspoon sea salt
2 tablespoons chopped parsley
3 garlic cloves, finely chopped
$\frac{1}{4}$ teaspoon smoked paprika

In a large mixing bowl stir the yeast into warm water. Stir until it has fully dissolved, then use your hands to mix in the flour, sugar, salt, garlic and chives until it forms a dough that easily comes away from the sides of the bowl. If the mix is a little dry and crumbly, add a splash of warm water.

Flour a work surface and firmly knead the dough until it is nice and elastic (around 10 minutes). Place in a lightly floured bowl or tray, loosely cover with lightly oiled clingfilm and leave in a warm place to rise until it has doubled in size (an airing cupboard for 30 minutes is perfect!).

Briefly re-knead the dough on a floured work surface and form into a ball. Cut the ball in half, then each half into half again. You should now have 4 pieces. Divide each piece into 4, so you end up with 16 pieces, each weighing 20–25g.

Lightly dust the work surface again with flour and firmly roll each piece to a walnut-sized ball. Line a large baking tray with baking parchment paper, then place on the dough balls, leaving enough space for them to prove and double in size. Cover with lightly oiled clingfilm and leave in a warm place for 30–40 minutes.

Preheat the oven to 180°C/Gas mark 4.

When the dough balls have proved, bake in the preheated oven for 15–20 minutes until they are golden brown.

Place the softened butter in a bowl and add the salt, parsley and finally the garlic, then beat with a wooden spoon until all ingredients are thoroughly mixed together.

Pile up the dough balls and dip into the butter. Enjoy them while they are hot.

Big Weekend Chill

The Ultimate Velvet Cauliflower and Macaroni Cheese

America, eat your heart out – this mac n' cheese rules! It's a melting pot of pure cheese bliss. You know those recipes in your cookbooks that are most used by all the stains and the pages sticking together? This, I guarantee, will become one of them! The topping makes this a very luxe version, and if you want to VIP it up, one of London's finest restaurants serves lobster in their opulent version.

serves **4-6**

1 large cauliflower, cut into florets
250g short-cut macaroni

For the cheese sauce
50g butter
50g plain flour
500ml milk
200ml double cream
200g mature farmhouse Cheddar, grated
1 teaspoon English mustard
2 free-range egg yolks
sea salt and freshly ground black pepper

For the velvet topping
50g butter
2 garlic cloves, finely chopped
50g fresh white breadcrumbs
50g Parmesan, grated
$1/4$ bunch of flat-leaf parsley, roughly chopped

Preheat the oven to 180°C/ Gas mark 4.

Blanch the cauliflower in a pan of boiling salted water until tender. Drain in a colander and refresh under cold running water. Leave to drain, then pat dry on kitchen paper to remove all water.

Cook the macaroni in plenty of boiling salted water until al dente, drain in a colander and refresh under cold running water. Leave to drain.

To make the cheese sauce, melt the butter in a pan over a medium heat. Add the flour and stir until it forms a paste, then cook gently for 3 minutes. Slowly beat in the milk until the sauce is smooth. Cook the sauce for a further 10 minutes, stirring gently, then stir in the cream and season.

Take the sauce off the heat and fold in the grated cheese and mustard. Quickly beat in the egg yolks and allow the sauce to cool to room temperature.

To make the topping, melt the butter in a frying pan over a medium heat until it starts to froth, then add the garlic and allow to soften for 2–3 minutes, but ensure that it does not burn. Finally, add the breadcrumbs and shake the pan to cover them in the butter mixture. Take the pan off the heat and add Parmesan and parsley.

Tip the macaroni and cauliflower into an ovenproof dish. Pour over the warm cheese sauce and finish with the breadcrumb topping. Bake in the oven for 15 minutes until bubbling and golden brown on top.

Salmon with Glazed Mozzarella and Tomato and Balsamic Chargrilled Chicory

Here the bitterness of the chicory is tempered by the caramelised sugar and balsamic vinegar. The showstopper in this dish is the best mustard sauce ever. I have been asked so many times for this recipe – it's so easy and is stunning with the salmon.

serves **4**

2 plum tomatoes
2 x 125g balls of mozzarella
4 x 150g salmon fillets
12 large fresh basil leaves

For the mustard sauce
2 tablespoons English mustard
2 tablespoons caster sugar
2 tablespoons white wine vinegar
8 tablespoons sunflower oil

For the balsamic chicory
4 heads of chicory
3 tablespoons olive oil
2 tablespoons balsamic vinegar
2 tablespoons caster sugar

Preheat the oven to 190C/ Gas mark 5. Line a baking tray with baking parchment.

Remove the eyes from the plum tomatoes and plunge into boiling water for 10 seconds, then into a bowl of iced water. Carefully remove the skin, then cut the tomatoes into quarters and deseed to make 8 petals. Slice the mozzarella ball into 8 slices 1cm thick.

Season the salmon fillets and layer on 3 large basil leaves, 2 tomato petals on top of the basil, season and finish with 2 slices of mozzarella. Place on the lined baking tray and cook in the preheated oven for 12–15 minutes until cooked and caramelised. If using a temperature probe, this should reach 60°C.

To make the sauce, place the mustard, sugar and vinegar in a bowl and whisk together slowly, adding the oil until it emulsifies together. Season to taste.

Split the chicory lengthways, rub in oil and balsamic vinegar and dust with the sugar. Place on a hot ridged grill pan, flat side down. Chargrill for 2–3 minutes until caramelised and tender.

To serve, place the chicory on a plate, with the salmon on top and finish with the mustard vinaigrette.

The Family Kitchen

Seared Scallops with Salad Cream and Rocket Mash

A beautiful, classy, bistro-style dish, yet so easy and effective.. Now I know what you're thinking... salad cream in mash? Try it to believe it! This has been one of my signature dishes for many years.

serves **4**

12 whole scallops, cleaned
2 tablespoons olive oil
sea salt and black pepper for
  seasoning
20g rocket leaves, to garnish
juice of $\frac{1}{2}$ lemon
2 tablespoons good-quality
  peppery olive oil, for dressing

For the rocket mash
4 large floury potatoes (Maris
  Piper are ideal), peeled and
  chopped
50g butter
5ml milk
2 tablespoons salad cream
50g rocket leaves
sea salt and freshly ground black
  pepper

Boil the potatoes in a saucepan of water over a medium heat until they are soft, then drain and mash them with the butter and milk until they are smooth and creamy. Season with a pinch of salt and pepper, then fold in the salad cream and rocket, place to one side, cover and keep warm.

Place a frying pan over a medium heat. Place the scallops in a bowl and gently coat with the olive oil and seasoning, then place in the hot frying pan and colour and caramelise on both sides for about 2 minutes, ensuring you do not overcook them.

Divide the mash into 4 bistro bowls, place 3 scallops on each bed of mash. Place the rocket garnish in a bowl and dress with fresh lemon juice. Grab a handful of leaves, roll into a ball and place on the scallops. Finish each bowl with a good glug of peppery olive oil.

Salt-crusted Roast Forerib with Caramelised Shallots and Golden Beets and Hot Horseradish

I used to make this when I lived in Israel. It's a beautiful, succulent beef theatre production, a 'showstopper' only for great mates, nearest and dearest. Make sure you use kosher or large salt crystals and take your beef out the fridge 2–3 hours before cooking, to allow it to get to room temperature.

serves **4**

3 tablespoons vegetable oil
2–2.5kg prime forerib, trimmed (around 3 ribs, French trim)

For the salt crust
350g (1 tub) coarse kosher sea salt, or large rock salt for grinding
2 free-range egg whites
1 tablespoon grated horseradish
1 tablespoon Worcestershire sauce
1 tablespoon English mustard powder
2 sprigs of rosemary leaves, roughly chopped
1 teaspoon thyme leaves
1 tablespoon water
1 teaspoon cracked black pepper

For the beetroot
1kg golden or red beetroot, washed and trimmed
4 tablespoons olive oil
1 tablespoons sea salt
1 teaspoon fresh thyme leaves, chopped
freshly ground black pepper

For the shallots
500g shallots, peeled
2 tablespoons vegetable oil
80g caster sugar

To serve
4cm (30g) piece fresh horseradish root
1 tablespoon white wine vinegar
284ml double cream
1 bunch of watercress, picked and washed

Preheat the oven to 190°C/Gas mark 5.

Thoroughly mix all salt crust ingredients together in a large bowl.

Heat a roasting tin over a high heat. Add the vegetable oil and allow to smoke, then carefully sear the forerib on all sides, ensuring you get a nice golden brown colour all over. Remove the roasting tin from heat.

Using your hands, pack the salt crust all over the top, patting down onto the beef. The crust should be around 1cm thick. Place in the preheated oven and cook for around 1$\frac{1}{2}$–2 hours, depending on how you like it cooked. If you have a meat thermometer or probe, 55°C produces perfect medium rare beef. Allow to rest to 30 minutes.

Place the beetroot in a roasting tin, splash and roll in olive oil, season with the salt and thyme leaves, then place in the oven until soft and tender (around 45 minutes), shaking the tin occasionally. Leave to cool, then gently rub off the skin using a piece of kitchen paper. Remove the root completely, then cut into 8 pieces and place in a bowl with a glug of olive oil. Cover with clingfilm and put to one side.

Place the shallots in a medium-sized saucepan and cover with water. Place over a medium heat, bring to the boil and blanch for 5 minutes, then drain in a colander and pat dry on kitchen paper. Place the shallots into a large frying pan, add the vegetable oil and sugar, then roll them around in the pan and turn with a spoon over a medium heat until golden and caramelised (around 15–20 minutes). Remove from the pan and place to one side.

Peel and grate the horseradish using a fine grater. Place in a bowl with the white wine vinegar. Place the cream in a bowl and whisk until semi-thick, gently fold in the horseradish and vinegar and season.

Gently remove the salt crust and carve the beef into slices 1cm thick. Place on a chopping board, and spoon over the caramelised shallots and beetroot. Serve with fresh horseradish cream and picked watercress.

Deep-filled Stilton and Leek Tart with Pear Waldorf Salad

A great brunch special, this has a glorious deep filling of leeks and Stilton. Any blue cheese is fine – you could use a salty Roquefort or a good Irish Cashel Blue. The fresh pears give a new twist to the Waldorf salad and make it a perfect companion to the tart. A great homemade centrepiece for family parties that will offend none and please all.

serves **4–6**

For the pastry
225g plain flour
pinch of sea salt
120g butter, chilled and diced
1 free-range egg yolk
4 tablespoons ice-cold water

For the filling
2 large leeks
40g butter
1 large red onion, sliced
4 large free-range eggs
1 large free-range egg yolk
200ml crème fraîche
200ml full-fat milk
1 teaspoon thyme leaves
250g Stilton
sea salt and freshly ground black pepper

For the salad
2 pears
juice of $\frac{1}{2}$ lemon
3 celery stalks, chopped
50g golden raisins
50g walnut halves
4 tablespoons mayonnaise
1 tablespoon Dijon mustard
$\frac{1}{2}$ bunch of watercress

To make the pastry, sift the flour and salt into a large mixing bowl, add the diced chilled butter and then start to work together using the tips of your fingers until the mix resembles breadcrumbs; do not overwork. Add in the egg yolk and then water to bring the mixture together – the pastry dough should have a smooth texture. Wrap in clingfilm and refrigerate for around 30 minutes.

Slice the leeks in half lengthways, then slice finely into half rounds. Heat the butter in a large frying pan, add the sliced onion and leeks and cook gently for 5–6 minutes until softened, season, drain in a colander and keep to one side to cool.

Preheat the oven to 170°C/ Gas mark 3$\frac{1}{2}$.

Take the pastry out of the fridge, lightly dust the work surface and roll out to a thickness of 5mm and until large enough to fit a 20cm x 5cm deep quiche tin. Carefully lower the pastry into the tin, pressing it into the edges and leaving any excess to overhang the tin; do not trim. Prick the base with a fork and place back in the fridge for 10 minutes. Remove from fridge, then line the pastry case with a 30cm circle of baking parchment and fill with baking beans (if you don't have baking beans, you can use rice). Bake in the oven for 20–25 minutes, to seal the pastry.

While the pastry case is cooking, place 3 whole eggs and 1 egg yolk into a bowl, add the crème fraîche, milk and thyme and whisk until all ingredients are incorporated together, season.

Crack the remaining egg into a bowl and whisk. Take the pastry case out of the oven and remove the baking beans or rice. While the pastry is still hot, brush generously with the egg (this ensures that there are no leaks). Place back in the oven for 5 minutes.

The Family Kitchen

Crumble the Stilton into a bowl, then add the leeks and onions and mix together. Tip the mixture into the pastry case, ensuring it is distributed evenly, then fill with the egg mixture.

Bake the quiche for 40–45 minutes or until set and golden brown.

Remove from the oven and trim off any excess overhanging pastry using a sharp serrated knife. Allow to rest for 10 minutes, then gently remove the quiche tin.

Peel and cut the pears in half, remove the core, then slice into thin strips lengthways. Squeeze over the lemon juice (this will stop the flesh from going brown) and place in a bowl. Add the celery, raisins and walnuts, then gently fold in the mayonnaise and Dijon mustard. Season and serve garnished with picked watercress leaves.

Virgin Mary

This is an 'innocent' drink, to be enjoyed by all the family. Drink it on a Sunday with the papers. Try dipping the damp rims of the glasses in celery salt, in the same way you would use salt with a margarita. Our neighbours, Marc and Lang, make an absolutely excellent 'not-so-virgin Mary'. You can do the same – simply add some Grey Goose Vodka and 'adult' this up!

serves **1**

1 teaspoon celery salt
dash of Worcestershire sauce
dash of Tabasco
$1/2$ teaspoon cracked black
   pepper
150ml tomato juice
juice of $1/2$ lemon
ice cubes
the leafy middle of the celery stalk
1 lime wedge

Wet the rim of a large (400ml) highball glass and dust in celery salt. Add a dash of Worcestershire sauce, Tabasco and black pepper to the bottom of the glass followed by the tomato and lemon juice.

Fill with ice and stir gently, then finish with the leafy stem of celery for stirring and a lime wedge garnish.

Away & At Play

The fondest memories of our childhood are holidays and quality time spent together as a family. So if the sun is shining jump in the motor and get picnicking.

How very British! A must for our picnics is the Big Boy Scotch Eggs (page 127), which are truly stunning. Try All-in-the-blender Tomato, Tarragon and Basil Chicken (page 118) – it's so easy and very, very tasty.

Now onto Train Journey Tapas – don't put up with overpriced and seriously under-flavoured shop-bought sarnies when you're off on a family adventure. The recipes here are really delicious and easy to eat on the move. Try The Perfect Pasty (page 140) – this will keep even the most discerning fuss-pots in the family happy! The Grab 'n' go Skewer Selection (page 134) is delish, as are the posh Mini Sandwich Stacks (page 133). All winners for eating on the hoof.

Lastly, our favourite chapter: The Kirby Gift Shop! We love to make things for people as it's much more personal than shop-bought gifts. Our family and friends appreciate the time we've invested in them and I'm sure yours will too. The best way to describe the feeling is to liken it to being presented with a card made by your kids – don't you cherish it all the more because you know it's come from the heart and not the shelf?

A great one to try is the Chocolate-dipped Honeycomb (page 148) or Amber's homemade and beautifully wrapped Jersey Cream Butter with Cornish Sea Salt (page 154) – so beautiful your friends won't want to unwrap it… until they smell the toast!

We've filled this chapter with our best smile-makers! So, go on, show your loved ones you care and that we're not too busy to spend a little time on them in this hectic rollercoaster we call life! Also, did I mention… the extra bonus of making your own gifts for people is it won't break the bank. Result!

All-in-the-Blender
Tomato, Tarragon and Basil Chicken

The ideal thing about this dish is that it travels really well and is great for picnics. I chose to do this recipe for the Golden Jubilee weekend broadcast on the BBC's *Saturday Kitchen* with my good mate Gregg Wallace. It's an amazingly easy peasy dish which still holds strong today. Perfect with a Jersey Royal potato salad with mustard-seed mayo.

serves **4**

1 litre chicken stock
4 corn-fed chicken breasts, wing bone trimmed and skinned
4 shallots
3 cloves of smoked garlic
$\frac{1}{4}$ bunch of tarragon, leaves only
$\frac{1}{4}$ bunch of basil, leaves only
400ml tomato ketchup
125ml sunflower oil
juice of $\frac{1}{2}$ lemon
1 tablespoon Worcestershire sauce
sea salt and freshly ground black pepper

Heat the stock in a medium saucepan, then add the chicken breasts and gently poach for 10–15 minutes until cooked through (if using a meat thermometer or probe, the temperature should reach 65–70°C, or prick with the tip of a knife to check the juices run clear). Transfer the chicken to a bowl. Retain the stock.

While the chicken is poaching, place the shallots, garlic, tarragon and basil in a blender and pulse until finely chopped. Add the tomato ketchup and slowly incorporate the oil, lemon juice, Worcestershire sauce and around 50ml of the chicken stock. Blend until combined and season to taste.

Place the tomato and herb dressing in a bowl. When the chicken is cooked, carefully drop into the dressing, making sure it is well covered. Leave to cool and marinate for 1 hour.

Once marinated, remove chicken from the bowl and serve with your favourite salad.

"The ideal thing about this dish is that it travels really well and is great for picnics."

The Family Kitchen

In-the-Pan Leek, Jersey Royal and Pea Frittata

I love picnics where people have really gone to town and made the effort. I make this dish a day before a planned trip and keep it chilled. This summer dish kept us sustained while watching on big screens in Hyde Park as our beautiful Kate and Wills tied the knot. We washed it down with a celebratory plastic flute of champers to toast the lovely couple.

serves **4**

8 baby leeks or 1 large leek, sliced into 1cm rounds
300g new-season Jersey Royal potatoes
8 free-range eggs
$\frac{1}{2}$ bunch of chives, chopped
$\frac{1}{2}$ bunch of mint, chopped
1 tablespoon olive oil
50g butter
2 banana shallots, finely sliced
50g washed baby spinach
160g frozen peas, defrosted
80g feta cheese, crumbled
sea salt and freshly ground black pepper

Cook the leeks in a pan of salted boiling water for 1–1$\frac{1}{2}$ minutes until just tender, then drain and refresh straight into cold water. Dry the leeks thoroughly.

Boil the potatoes in salted water for 10–12 minutes until tender, drain and leave to cool. Once potatoes have cooled enough for you to handle, cut into 1cm-thick slices.

Crack the eggs into a large bowl and whisk until well beaten, then add in the chopped chives and mint and season. Heat a large frying pan (around 30cm) over a medium-high heat and add the olive oil and butter. Once the butter starts to froth, add the potatoes and shallots and fry until golden brown, around 5–10 minutes, ensuring you shake the pan regularly.

Meanwhile, preheat the grill.

Add the baby spinach to the pan and leave to wilt for about 30 seconds, then add the peas and mix. Pour in the egg mixture, making sure it is evenly distributed. Leave on heat for around 2 minutes without moving until it starts to set, then arrange the leeks nicely over the top and crumble over the feta.

Place the frying pan under the grill and cook for around 3–4 minutes or until the frittata is set and cooked through. Leave to to cool, then cut into wedges and serve.

Hot Smoked Salmon with Crispy New Potatoes

The colours of this dish shout summer – it really is so fresh and zingy. The hot smoked salmon flaked through the crispy potatoes and crème fraîche dressing is an absolute stunner.

serves **4**

300g new potatoes
3 tablespoons olive oil
1 tablespoon fresh thyme leaves
30g white breadcrumbs
300g hot-smoked salmon
1 tablespoon horseradish, grated
juice of $\frac{1}{2}$ lemon
150g crème fraîche
1 tablespoon good-quality olive
   oil, for dressing
2 lemons, cut into quarters,
   to garnish
handful of watercress, to garnish
freshly ground black pepper

Preheat the oven to 180°C/
Gas mark 4.

Place the potatoes in a saucepan, cover with salted water and parboil on a medium heat until three-quarters cooked. Drain and, when cool enough to handle, cut in half lengthways, place in a roasting tray with the oil and fresh thyme. Mix thoroughly, season and roast in the oven for 15 minutes until crispy. Add the breadcrumbs and gently fold together, then place back in the oven for a further 10 minutes until golden brown.

Take out of the oven, leave in the roasting tray and allow to cool to room temperature. Gently flake the smoked salmon over the roasted new potatoes.

Place on a large flat serving plate. Stir the horseradish and lemon juice into the crème fraîche and liberally drizzle over the top of the salmon. Finish with the watercress and a glug of good-quality olive oil and black pepper. Serve with lemon wedges.

Watermelon, Peach and Feta Salad with Roasted Sunflower Seeds

This dish takes me back to a family holiday in the south of France. We quickly learnt that eating out wasn't going to happen every night – I couldn't believe the prices! Luckily, there was a lovely roadside market where I would buy beautiful, juicy, flat mountain peaches, watermelons and other lovely sun-ripened fruits and veggies. I made this dish and we now have it every time we have a picnic. Needless to say, the family ate well during that holiday and said it was one of their best. I needed another one when we returned...

serves **4**

¼ large watermelon, peeled
2 peaches
125g feta cheese
25g baby spinach leaves
30g sunflower seeds
1 lime
glug of olive oil
breadsticks, to serve

Preheat the oven to 180°C/ Gas mark 4.

Dice the watermelon into 2cm cubes and place in a bowl.

Cut the peaches into 8 pieces, remove the stones and add to the watermelon. Crumble the feta over the top, then add the spinach leaves.

Place the sunflower seeds on a roasting tray and brown in the oven for 5–10 minutes. Sprinkle over watermelon, peaches, feta and spinach.

Gently spoon into preserving jars. When you are ready to enjoy, squeeze over fresh lime and olive oil. Serve with homemade breadsticks.

The Family Kitchen

Tomato and Goat's Cheese Tart

This is a very easy and tasty summer dish. The key to this is to use the best tomatoes you can find. Nice ripe ones which are a lovely red with bags of flavour. I never keep my tomatoes in the fridge as this makes them tasteless.

serves **4**

250g puff pastry
3 plum tomatoes or vine-ripened
  tomatoes
100g soft goat's cheese log
  (rindless), at room temperature
150ml double cream
½ bunch of chives, finely
  chopped
30g baby watercress
1 tablespoon good-quality olive oil
1 tablespoon balsamic vinegar
50g walnut pieces
sea salt and freshly ground black
  pepper

Preheat the oven to 190°C/
Gas mark 5. Line 2 baking trays
with baking parchment.

Roll out the pastry to a thickness
of 5mm and cut 4 circles about
12cm in diameter. Transfer to one
of the lined baking trays, top with
the second sheet of paper and
the second baking tray (this
prevents uneven rising). Bake in
the oven for 30–35 minutes.
When golden brown, transfer to
a cooling rack and allow to cool.

Slice the tomatoes very thinly
and arrange on top of the pastry,
layering the slices in a circle, then
season.

Place the goat's cheese in a
mixing bowl and mash with a
fork, then whisk and beat in the
cream until you get a texture like
soft ice cream (this can be done
in a food processor). Add the
chives to the goat's cheese,
season and then spoon or pipe
the mixture on top of the
tomatoes.

Place the watercress in a bowl
and dress with the olive oil,
vinegar and walnuts, then pile on
top of the tart and serve.

"This is a very easy and tasty summer dish."

The Family Kitchen

Baby Gem, Crispy Parma Ham and Pine nut Salad with Roquefort Sauce

A sunny picnic salad that can be put together at the last minute. I also put this out for our BBQs and I catch each and every one of my family having a sneaky pick at it, so by the time the meat is cooked, there is hardly any left! You'll have some Roquefort sauce left but it will keep well in the fridge.

serves 4

4 free-range eggs
8 slices of Parma ham
50g pine nuts
2 slices of medium-cut white
   bread
2 tablespoons vegetable oil
100g Roquefort cheese
284ml double cream
4 Baby Gem lettuces
50g Parmesan cheese, grated
freshly ground black pepper

Place the eggs in a saucepan of water and hard boil them for 8–10 minutes, then refresh under cold running water. Carefully peel the eggs, pat dry, then roughly chop and place in a bowl to one side.

Place the Parma ham slices on a baking tray and grill for 2 minutes on each side until crispy.

Place the pine nuts on a baking tray and grill and brown for about 2 minutes, shaking all the time for an even colour.

Cut the sliced bread into croutons, 2 x 2cm. Place a frying pan over a medium heat, add the oil and allow to heat. Once hot, fry the croutons, turning them with a wooden spoon until golden brown, for around 5 minutes. Place on kitchen paper to drain and season.

To make the sauce, place the Roquefort in a glass bowl and mash with a fork until soft. Gently whisk in the cream and season with black pepper to taste (this can be done in a food processor).

Finally, split the lettuce lengthways, remove the root, wash and pat dry, then place flat side up on a large serving dish. Add the chopped egg. Break the crispy Parma ham into shards and place on top, then sprinkle with the croutons and pine nuts. At the last minute, finish with the Roquefort sauce and grated Parmesan.

Big Boy Scotch Eggs

How do you eat yours? I love mine with HP Sauce or salad cream. They work really well with English mustard too! If you want a lovely runny yolk, pay special attention and love to the cooking time of your eggs.

serves **4**

7 free-range eggs
1 large Bramley cooking apple
25g butter
1 tablespoon chopped thyme
200g good-quality sausage meat
200g minced pork
1 tablespoon chopped sage
1 tablespoon chopped parsley
1 tablespoon wholegrain mustard
50g flour
170g panko breadcrumbs
2 tablespoons dried sage
oil, for deep-fat frying
sea salt and freshly ground black pepper

Place 4 of the eggs in a saucepan, cover with cold water and bring to the boil for 4 minutes, then remove and immediately refresh in ice-cold water. When the eggs are completely cold, peel them and pat dry, then leave to one side.

Peel and core the cooking apple and cut into 5mm cubes. Add the butter to a frying pan and place over a medium heat. When the butter starts to froth, add the apple and thyme and cook for just 1 minute, shaking the pan until the apple just starts to soften. Tip the apple on to kitchen paper and pat dry.

Place the sausage meat, pork mince, sage, parsley and mustard in a large bowl, season and mix well. Add the apple and thyme and mix gently, taking care not to break up the apple.

Place a 30cm square of clingfilm on the table and lightly oil. Place a quarter of the sausage meat mixture (around 125g) in the middle and spread out, using your fingers, until it is large enough to encase the egg. Place the egg in the middle and, using the clingfilm, shape and mould the sausage meat around the egg, making a smooth shape and ensuring the egg is sealed in. Wrap in the clingfilm. Repeat the process with the remaining eggs and leave to chill in the fridge for 1 hour.

For the breadcrumb coating, crack the remaining 3 eggs into a bowl and beat. Place the flour in another bowl and season, and mix the breadcrumbs and dried sage in a third bowl.

Remove the clingfilm from the chilled Scotch eggs, then roll first in the flour, then the egg and lastly the breadcrumbs; repeat this process again to ensure a good coating.

Heat the oil to 160°C. Place one egg in the deep-fat fryer at a time and cook for 6–7 minutes until crisp and golden. Remove from the oil and drain on kitchen paper. Repeat this process for the remaining eggs.

Season, leave to cool and then serve.

Pomegranate Couscous

You can really jazz up a staple ingredient like couscous, and this is a great suggestion. This also works well with leftover leg of lamb shredded into it with flat-leaf parsley and pickled lemons. Handsome!

serves 4

200g couscous
300ml vegetable stock
3 tablespoons olive oil
1 large pomegranate
2 tablespoons mint leaves, roughly chopped
2 tablespoons coriander, roughly chopped
1 bunch of spring onions, chopped
30g sunflower seeds
30g dried cranberries
zest and juice of 1 lemon
freshly ground black pepper

Place the couscous in a large bowl. Place the vegetable stock in a saucepan and bring to the boil. Pour the boiling stock over the couscous, cover with clingfilm and leave to cool slightly. When the couscous has cooled, add a tablespoon of the olive oil (this will help to separate the grains), then use a fork to fluff up the couscous, separating it out until there are no large lumps left in the bowl.

Cut the pomegranate in half, then hold the pomegranate seed side down over a bowl and carefully hit the back of the pomegranate with a spoon. The seeds will all fall into the bowl. Repeat this process with the other half, ensuring you remove any white pith from the bowl.

Throw the pomegranate seeds, mint, coriander, spring onions, sunflower seeds and dried cranberries into the couscous. Then finally add the lemon zest, juice and the remaining olive oil, mix thoroughly and season with pepper.

The Family Kitchen

Hand-Tied Lemon Drizzle Bars with Fresh Raspberries

Lemon drizzle, yum! Try it with fresh raspberries and hand-tie the bars in baking parchment so you don't get sticky fingers. If you want to be fancy, you can crystallise some lemon peel to decorate the tops of the bars.

makes **14** *bars*

10g butter, for greasing
1 vanilla pod
5 free-range eggs
80g melted butter
100ml double cream
zest of 3 lemons
juice of 1 lemon
300g caster sugar
pinch of sea salt
240g plain flour
½ teaspoon baking powder
1 punnet of fresh raspberries,
  to serve

For the glaze
juice of 3 lemons
300g icing sugar

Preheat the oven to 180°C/ Gas mark 4. Lightly butter a 30 x 20cm baking tin and line with baking parchment.

Split the vanilla pod and scrape the seeds into a large mixing bowl, then whisk together with the eggs, melted butter, cream, lemon zest, lemon juice, sugar and salt.

Sift the flour and baking powder into the egg mixture and whisk thoroughly until you have a smooth batter. Pour into the lined tin, place in the oven and bake for 35–45 minutes. To test, insert a knife into the cake; the blade should come out clean.

Remove the cake from the oven, turn out on a wire rack and leave to cool.

To make the glaze, mix together the lemon juice and the icing sugar and whisk until smooth.

Cut the cake into 8 x 3cm bars and leave on the wire rack. Liberally spoon the glaze over the bars until all of it has been used.

Wrap the bars in baking parchment and tie with raffia. Serve with a punnet of fresh raspberries.

Perfect Picnic Possets

The lavender sugar in the shortbread gives it a really pretty finish and a delicate scent. A nice variation of this is to spoon some passionfruit curd into the jars, then top with the lemon posset.

serves **4**

3 lemons, ideally unwaxed
600ml double cream
1 vanilla pod, seeds reserved
175g caster sugar

For the shortbread
150g plain flour
100g butter, cubed and softened
50g lavender sugar, plus 10g for
    sprinkling
2 drops vanilla extract

Zest or finely grate the lemons into a bowl, add the double cream and vanilla seeds and gently whisk together. Pour the mixture into a medium saucepan and heat slowly over a low heat to just below boiling, then add the caster sugar and dissolve. Stir continuously over low-medium heat for 3 minutes, bringing slowly to the boil. Take off the heat, place to one side and allow to cool (around 20 minutes).

Squeeze the lemons through a sieve into a bowl, then whisk in the cooled cream mixture. Pour carefully into jam jars and seal (or use glasses) and place in the fridge to set.

To make the shortbread, tip the flour into a large mixing bowl, add in the butter and rub together until the mixture looks like fine breadcrumbs. Fold in the lavender sugar and the vanilla extract and work the mixture with your hands until it forms a ball.

Continue kneading the biscuit dough until it is smooth and the bowl sides are clean. Wrap the dough in clingfilm and chill in the fridge for 30 minutes.

Preheat the oven to 130°C/ Gas mark ½.

Remove the dough from the fridge and allow it to get to room temperature so it's workable. Lightly flour a work surface and roll out the dough until it is about 1cm thick, 24cm in length and 10cm wide. Cut out rectangles about 3cm in width (this mixture should make 8 biscuits). Transfer to a baking-parchment-lined baking tray.

Bake the shortbreads in the oven for 30 minutes until they are very pale gold in colour, remove to a wire rack and sprinkle with some lavender sugar whilst they are still warm. Leave to cool before serving with the possets.

The Family Kitchen

Mini Blueberry Loaf Cakes

You can buy great disposable mini loaf moulds in good supermarkets or kitchenware shops. It's worth getting disposables so your cakes can stay in their moulds until it's time to eat. This is a great way of getting the super-fruit blueberries into the younger ones' tums.

makes 8–10 cakes

175g butter, at room temperature
175g caster sugar
3 free-range eggs
225g self-raising flour
1 teaspoon baking powder
375g fresh blueberries
2 teaspoons vanilla extract
60ml soured cream
300g cream cheese
100g icing sugar
1 punnet of fresh blueberries,
  to garnish

Preheat the oven to 180°C/ Gas mark 4. Cut strips of parchment paper measuring 24 x 4.5cm to line the mini loaf moulds, leaving an overhang of 2cm each side (this will help pull the cakes out of the moulds later on).

Beat the butter and caster sugar together in a bowl until pale, light and fluffy. Beat the eggs together in a separate bowl, then slowly add into the butter mixture a little at a time. Sift the flour and baking powder together, then carefully fold the flour into the egg mixture, taking care not to overmix.

Gently crush half the blueberries with the back of a spoon. Add to the mixture along with the vanilla extract, 4 teaspoons of the soured cream and the remaining whole blueberries and combine thoroughly.

Divide the mix between the moulds, filling them just over halfway. Place on a baking tray and bake in the preheated oven for 30–40 minutes. Use the tip of a knife to check if they are cooked – the tip should come out cleanly. Remove from the oven and leave to cool in their moulds.

Using a whisk, beat the cream cheese, icing sugar and remaining soured cream in a bowl until the mixture is smooth and creamy.

Once the loaf cakes are cooled, carefully spread or pipe the tops with the cream cheese mixture and decorate with the fresh blueberries. Place in the fridge to firm up before transporting.

Mini Sandwich Stacks

When I was cooking at the Mansion House, the Lord Mayor of London's official residence, this was how we served posh bite-sized triple-decker sarnies. I've given you three varieties, opposite, to enjoy. This is a great idea for children's parties too.

serves 4–6
(2 of each flavour triple-decker sandwich)

The Family Kitchen

Tuna and Smoked Salmon

2 tablespoons soft cream cheese
6 slices of medium-cut brown
    bread
200g smoked salmon
100g tuna, drained

1 tablespoon mayonnaise
sea salt and freshly ground black
    pepper

Spread a quarter of the cream cheese on one slice of the bread and lay half the smoked salmon on top. Spread the next slice of bread with another quarter of the cream cheese and lay on top, spread side down.

Mix the tuna and mayonnaise together in a bowl, season and spread half on top of the smoked salmon sandwich. Finish with another layer of bread.

Repeat the layering process to make a second triple-decker salmon and tuna sandwich. Place under a clean, damp cloth to keep fresh.

Egg and Mature Cheddar

2 free-range eggs, hard boiled
4 tablespoons mayonnaise
150g mature Cheddar cheese,
    grated
1/2 bunch of spring onions, finely
    chopped
6 slices of medium-cut white
    bread
sea salt and freshly ground black
    pepper

Fork the eggs into a bowl, fold in half the mayonnaise, season and mix.

Place the grated cheese in a bowl, add the remaining mayonnaise and chopped spring onions. Season and mix together.

Spread half the cheese and onion mix on one slice of bread, top with another slice of bread and spread half of the egg mayonnaise on top of this. Season with more black pepper, then top with the final slice of bread.

Repeat the layering process to make a second triple-decker egg and cheese sandwich. Place under a clean, damp cloth to keep fresh.

Beef Horseradish and Red Leicester

1 teaspoon horseradish
5 tablespoons mayonnaise
4 slices of medium-cut white
    bread
4 thin slices of cooked beef
40g watercress
2 slices of medium-cut brown
    bread
150g farmhouse red Leicester
    cheese, grated
1/2 onion, finely chopped

Mix the horseradish and 2 tablespoons of mayonnaise in a small bowl, then spread a quarter over one slice of white bread. Top with 2 slices of beef and sprinkle on some watercress. Spread one slice of brown bread with another quarter of the horseradish mayonnaise and place spread side down on the beef.

Mix the cheese, chopped onion and remaining mayonnaise together in a small bowl and season. Spread half of this mixture on top of the beef sandwich and top with a slice of white bread.

Repeat the layering process to make a second triple-decker beef and red Leicester sandwich. Place under a clean, damp cloth to keep fresh.

To serve, take all of the sandwiches and use a sharp serrated knife to remove the crusts. Cut into square quarters, skewer to hold together and serve.

Grab n' go Skewer Selection

Of course you don't have to make all of these different options, but if you feel like making the effort, it will be appreciated by all. These go down a storm in our city grab n' go restaurants.

all recipes serve **4**

Coconut and Lime Chicken

2 skinless chicken breasts
200ml coconut milk
$\frac{1}{2}$ red chilli, chopped and
    deseeded
4cm piece of ginger, peeled
1 clove garlic
$\frac{1}{2}$ tablespoon clear honey
1 tablespoon ground turmeric
$\frac{1}{4}$ bunch of coriander
zest and juice of 1 lime
8 x 15cm bamboo skewers
2 tablespoons olive oil

Cut each chicken breast into 4 long strips and place in a bowl.

Place the coconut milk, chilli, ginger, garlic, honey, turmeric, coriander and lime zest and juice in a food processor. Blend until all ingredients are well combined. Pour over the chicken, cover with clingfilm and leave to marinate in the fridge for minimum of 4 hours (overnight is best).

Soak the skewers in a bowl of water for about an hour (this will prevent them from burning during cooking). Preheat the oven to 180°C/Gas mark 4.

Remove the chicken from the marinade and drain, then thread one piece of chicken onto one end of each skewer.

Heat a frying pan over a medium heat and add the oil. When the oil is hot, place the skewers in the pan and colour evenly on both sides (be careful they don't burn). Once all the chicken is golden brown, place in a roasting tray and finish cooking in the oven for 6–7 minutes or until cooked through.

Sesame Salmon

200g skinless salmon fillet
8 x 15cm bamboo skewers
50g sesame seeds
2 tablespoons olive oil

For the marinade
1 tablespoon each of soy sauce
    and mirin or sweet sherry
1 teaspoon each of
    Worcestershire sauce, crushed
    ginger, crushed garlic and dark
    brown sugar

Cut the salmon fillets into 2cm cubes. Combine the soy, mirin, Worcestershire sauce, ginger, garlic and sugar in a bowl and stir until the sugar dissolves. Add the salmon and leave to marinate in the fridge for around an hour.

Soak the skewers in a bowl of water for about an hour. Preheat the oven to 180°C/Gas mark 4.

Drain the salmon from the marinade, then thread onto one end of the skewers – there should be around 3 pieces per skewer. Put the sesame seeds in a bowl or on a plate, then coat the salmon skewers by turning them in the seeds and gently patting them in place.

The Family Kitchen

Lemon and Thyme Halloumi with Red Pepper

250g halloumi
1 large red pepper, deseeded
zest and juice of 1 lemon
50ml olive oil
1 garlic clove, chopped
$\frac{1}{4}$ bunch of coriander, chopped
8 x 15cm bamboo skewers

Heat a frying pan over a medium heat and add the olive oil. When oil is hot, add the skewers to the pan and colour evenly on both sides (be careful they don't burn).

Once all skewers are coloured, place on a roasting tray and finish cooking in the oven for 4–5 minutes or until cooked through.

Cut the halloumi and pepper into 2cm cubes, then place in a bowl. Add the zest and juice of the lemon, olive oil, garlic and chopped coriander. Marinate in the fridge for around 1 hour.

Soak the skewers in a bowl of water for about an hour. Preheat the grill to its highest setting.

Thread the skewers with alternate cubes of pepper and halloumi – around 2 pieces of each per skewer. Cover the exposed end of each skewer with a piece of foil to prevent burning under the grill. Place the skewers on a baking tray underneath the hot grill and cook for 1–2 minutes or until the cheese starts to colour, then turn over and repeat for the other side.

Remove from the grill and leave to cool slightly, then remove the foil and serve.

Tiny Tapas Tasting Pots

Perfect little tasters of wonderful flavours.
If you're an anchovy addict like me, you must try
the anchovy and potato salad. It is so moreish!

all recipes serve **4**

Smoked Spicy Paprika Peppers

300ml olive oil
1 large red pepper
1 yellow pepper
1 green pepper
2 large green chillies
2 teaspoons smoked paprika
2 cloves smoked garlic, thinly
　sliced
1 teaspoon coriander seeds
150ml sherry vinegar
$1/2$ bunch of flat-leaf parsley,
　chopped
sea salt and freshly ground black
　pepper

Preheat the oven to 200°C/
Gas mark 6.

Rub 1 tablespoon of the olive
oil into the peppers and chillies,
place on a roasting tray and
roast for 12–15 minutes until
the peppers are coloured and
blistered. Remove from oven and
place in a large bowl, cover with
clingfilm and leave to cool.

Pour the remaining oil into a
medium saucepan and whisk the
paprika, garlic and coriander
seeds into the cold oil. Heat the
oil very gently for 5 minutes, then
remove from the heat and leave
to cool and infuse.

Once the peppers are cool
enough to handle, cut them in
half and remove the core and
seeds. Peel off the skin, cut the
flesh into strips 2cm wide and
place back in the bowl. Peel the
chillies and remove the seeds,
then chop finely and add to
the peppers.

Pass the oil through a sieve over
the top of the peppers. Add the
sherry vinegar and chopped
parsley, then mix well and
season.

Oven-Dried Cherry Tomatoes, Feta and Fresh Oregano

1 punnet each of red and yellow
　cherry tomatoes
$1/2$ bunch of oregano
3 garlic cloves, finely chopped
1 teaspoon caster sugar
180g feta cheese
150ml extra-virgin olive oil
sea salt and freshly ground black
　pepper

Preheat the oven to 100°C/
Gas mark $1/2$. Line a large baking
tray with baking parchment.

Cut the tomatoes in half and
place on the lined baking tray.
Strip the leaves from half the
oregano and chop, then mix with
the garlic and sprinkle over the
tomatoes. Season with the sugar,
sea salt and black pepper, mixing
gently to ensure the tomatoes are
completely covered. Place in the
oven to dry out and shrink to half
their size – this takes $1^1/2$–2 hours.

Once dried, remove from the
oven and leave to cool.

Dice the feta into 1cm cubes
and place in a bowl. Pick the
remaining leaves from the
oregano and add to the cheese.
Add the tomatoes to the bowl
and pour over the oil. Mix really
gently and leave to marinate for
a couple of hours, then serve.

Smoked Anchovy Caper and Lemon Potato Salad

300g new potatoes
50g smoked or marinated
　anchovies, finely chopped
25g capers
zest and juice of 1 lemon
$1/2$ bunch of flat-leaf parsley,
　chopped
50ml olive oil

Cut the new potatoes in half,
place in a saucepan, cover with
water and bring to the boil.
Cook until tender.

In a large mixing bowl add the
chopped anchovies, capers,
lemon zest and juice, chopped
parsley and olive oil and mix well
using a whisk.

When the potatoes are cooked,
drain in a colander. Add to the
mixing bowl while still hot and
mix well with the anchovy
dressing. Leave to cool in the
dressing, chill and serve.

Away & At Play

Mini Pudding Shots

These assorted puds in mini pots are great for eating on the go. Alternatively, they make a good dinner party option when served in something glam. But however you choose to serve them, they will impress all!

serves **4**

Chocolate and Orange Pots

300ml double cream
1 vanilla pod
zest and juice of 1 orange
200g best-quality dark cooking
  chocolate
2 large egg yolks
20g butter

Place the cream, vanilla pod and orange zest in a saucepan over a medium heat. Remove from the heat just before the cream boils and leave to infuse for 5 minutes.

Smash up the chocolate and add to the cream, stirring until all the chocolate has melted and you have a nice silky smooth consistency. Now add the egg yolks, orange juice and butter. Stir until the butter has completely melted, then remove the vanilla pod. Pour into the mini pots and place into the fridge to set.

Remove the pots from fridge about 30 minutes before serving.

Raspberry and Lemon Cheesecake Pots

6 digestive biscuits
25g butter
250g fresh raspberries
zest and juice of 1 lemon
2 tablespoons caster sugar
125g mascarpone cheese
150g full-fat cream cheese
4 tablespoons double cream
$\frac{1}{2}$ vanilla pod, seeds reserved
4 tablespoons icing sugar

Crush the digestive biscuits either in a bowl or a food processor. Melt the butter and mix with the biscuits. Divide between 4 pots and press down firmly. Place in the fridge to set.

Reserve 4 raspberries for garnishing, and place the remaining berries in a small saucepan with the lemon juice and sugar. Heat gently for around 3 minutes until all the sugar has dissolved. Leave to go cold.

In a bowl, mix together the mascarpone, cream cheese, lemon zest, cream, vanilla seeds and icing sugar, then using a whisk combine thoroughly until you have a light fluffy mixture. Spoon this mixture into a piping bag.

The Family Kitchen

Mini Strawberry Trifles

3 mini strawberry Swiss rolls
250g fresh strawberries
1 packet of strawberry jelly
200g readymade custard
250ml double cream
hundreds and thousands

Cut the Swiss rolls into slices
1cm thick. Line the 4 pudding
pots with the slices to just under
halfway up the pots.

Reserve 4 of the strawberries for
garnishing, and roughly dice the
remaining berries into 1cm cubes.
Divide between the pots.
Make up the jelly according to the
packet instructions, then pour
over the sponge just enough to
cover. Place in the fridge to set.

Remove the pots from fridge
and pour over the custard –
you should add enough to come
three-quarters of the way up
the pot. Return to the fridge for
30 minutes.

Whip the cream in a bowl, then
spoon it into a piping bag and
pipe the cream over the trifles.
Garnish with hundreds and
thousands and the reserved
strawberries.

Remove the biscuit pots from fridge
and add a tablespoon of the
raspberry mixture to each pot.
Pipe the cream cheese mix
between the pots, then finally
top with the rest of the raspberry
mixture and finish with a
fresh raspberry.

The Perfect Pasty – half sweet, half savoury

I am not even going to begin to pretend I am fully versed in the heritage of the humble pasty, but what I do know is that it originally used to have two fillings – savoury at one end, and sweet at the other. Made as lunch for miners, the pastry crimping on the edge was for the miners to hold whilst they ate, as their hands would have been very dirty. Whatever the history, this is my idea of food heaven!

serves **6**

For the pastry
600g plain flour
pinch of sea salt
150g butter, diced and chilled
150g lard, diced and chilled
1 free-range egg, beaten
150ml ice-cold water
2 free-range egg yolks, beaten, to glaze
1 teaspoon sea salt, to season
1 teaspoon caster sugar

For the savoury filling
180g beef skirt or chuck steak, finely chopped
1 large white onion, finely chopped
1 large potato, cut into wedges and thinly sliced
100g swede, cut into wedges and thinly sliced
glug of Worcestershire sauce
sea salt and freshly ground black pepper

For the sweet filling
30g butter
3 large cooking apples, peeled, cored and roughly chopped
75g caster sugar
1 vanilla pod, seeds reserved
½ teaspoon chopped fresh thyme leaves

To make the pastry, sift the flour into a large mixing bowl. Add the pinch of salt, butter and lard and gently rub together using your fingertips until you have a fine crumb-like mixture. Add the beaten egg and a little cold water to form a dough. Divide the dough into 6 equal balls, wrap in clingfilm and leave in the fridge for 30 minutes.

Preheat the oven to 180°C/ Gas mark 4. Line a baking tray with baking parchment.

Thoroughly mix together all the savoury ingredients in a bowl, season and place to one side.

To make the sweet filling, melt the butter in a saucepan. Add the apples, sugar, vanilla seeds and thyme leaves. Cook gently for 7–10 minutes until the fruit is stewed and still chunky. Place to one side and allow to cool.

On a lightly floured work surface, roll the balls of pastry into circles approximately 22cm in diameter (use a plate to cut around for a perfect circle). Re-roll the trimmings and cut six 11 x 1cm strips.

Spoon the savoury filling into the bottom right-hand corner of your pastry circles and the sweet filling into the bottom left-hand quarter; don't be tempted to overfill. Divide the 2 fillings with the pastry strips, making sure to leave a 2cm border around the edges to seal the pastry.

Glaze all around the edges and the centre strip with the egg yolk, then fold the top half of the circles over to enclose the fillings. Seal the edges, either twisting for the classic look or crimping with a fork. Make sure you press down in the middle of the pasty with the back of a knife to seal so that the two fillings don't leak together when cooking.

Slide the pasties onto the lined baking tray. Glaze the top of the pasties with the remaining egg yolk. Sprinkle a little cracked sea salt on the savoury side and caster sugar on the sweet side. Bake for approximately 40 minutes until golden brown. Re-glaze halfway through cooking for a gorgeous deep colour.

The Family Kitchen

Mozzarella and Med Veg Wedge

Italy on a plate! This really is a thing of beauty when you cut into it. I used to make these years ago, but it's still a noteworthy recipe (although please note that it does need chilling in the fridge overnight). Try cutting the wedge, brushing with olive oil and slamming it on a hot ridged grill pan.

serves **6**

6 tablespoons olive oil
2 red, 2 green and 2 orange peppers, quartered, cored and deseeded
2 large courgettes, sliced 1cm thick lengthways
2 aubergines, sliced 1cm thick lengthways
1 large ball Pugliese bread (around 800g)
2 garlic cloves, chopped
3 tablespoons smooth pesto sauce
2 x 125g mozzarella, sliced into 1cm rounds
1 bunch of basil, leaves picked
sea salt and freshly ground black pepper
mayonnaise, to serve

Place a ridged grill pan or frying pan over a medium heat, add 1 tablespoon of olive oil and allow to smoke. Gently add the peppers and chargrill or pan fry until tender and soft, then drain on kitchen paper. Repeat with the courgettes and aubergines. (If your pan is not very large, you may need to cook them in batches.)

Using a serrated knife, cut off the top third of the loaf. Using your hands, gently remove the soft dough from inside the loaf and the lid, leaving you with the crust intact (discard the bread or keep to make breadcrumbs).

Rub the inside of the loaf case with 2 tablespoons of olive oil, the garlic and the pesto sauce. Fill the loaf case with layers of aubergines, courgette, peppers and mozzarella, adding seasoning and scattering fresh basil leaves between each layer. Take the layers higher than the loaf, as you will compress them down into the bread.

Place the bread 'lid' on top and wrap the whole loaf tightly with several layers of clingfilm. Place the wrapped loaf on a baking tray, place another baking tray over the top and weigh down with a large casserole dish or a similar heavy weight to press overnight in the fridge.

Remove the clingfilm and cut into wedges; serve with mayonnaise.

The Family Kitchen

Vietnamese Prawn Rolls

Full on flavour, yet light on the calories. These are a great on-the-hoof gap filler. You can buy rice paper sheets in most Asian grocers. Work quickly when making these. They are a little fiddly, but worth the effort. These are so diverse they could have sat in any of the chapters in this book.

serves **4**

sesame oil
25g vermicelli rice noodles
4 round sheets of rice paper, 21cm in diameter
16 large cooked peeled prawns
1/4 bunch of mint
1/4 bunch of coriander
1/2 carrot, cut into thin strips
1/4 cucumber, cut into thin strips
2 spring onions, finely sliced
50g cashew nuts, toasted and chopped

For the dipping sauce
25g demerara sugar
1/2 red chilli, deseeded and finely chopped
1/2 teaspoon ginger, finely chopped
100ml soy sauce
1/2 teaspoon sesame seeds

To make the sauce, mix the sugar, chilli, ginger and soy sauce together in a small saucepan. Bring to the boil and leave to reduce by half (around 5 minutes). Remove from the heat and pour the sauce into a bowl with the sesame seeds. Keep to one side.

Oil some 30 x 30cm squares of baking parchment with sesame oil.

Place the noodles into a bowl and cover with boiling water. Leave for 4 minutes to soften, then drain and refresh under cold running water.

Submerge one sheet of rice paper in a large bowl of warm water for approximately 10 seconds to soften, remove and quickly pat dry on a clean tea towel. Carefully place the sheet on a square of oiled baking parchment. Place 4 prawns down the centre, then place 3 torn mint leaves and 3 torn coriander leaves on top, followed by a quarter of the noodles, carrot, cucumber and spring onion. Finish with a sprinkle of cashew nuts.

Roll the rice paper into a spring-roll shape, tucking in the ends. Roll in the parchment paper and gently twist the ends for transporting. Repeat with all your rolls then place in the fridge until needed. Serve with the dipping sauce.

"Full on flavour, yet light on the calories. These are a great on-the-hoof gap filler."

We love making these homemade treats
that we give as gifts to friends and family.
And they all love them too!

On the top shelf, opposite, you'll find Funky
Herb Oil (page 146); Seville Orange Marmalade
(page 155); and Honey and Pecan Biscuit Tubes
(page 148). On the shelf below, there's more of
the Funky Herb Oil; and our Chocolate-Dipped
Honeycomb (page 148). Below that, there's
Shortbread Stars (page 149); Glittered Salted
Caramel (page 149); Jersey Cream Butter
with Cornish Sea Salt (page 154); and our
Do-it-Yourself Brownie Kit (page 152).
And on the bottom shelf, there's Punchy
Piccalilli (page 147), Rhubarb, Ginger and
Vanilla Pod Jam (page 154); and Onion and
Thyme Chutney (page 146).

Have a go and give one of the nicest gifts
you can give!

Onion and Thyme Chutney

This chutney, some beautiful Montgomery Cheddar and a bottle of quality red – job done!

Fills **4** small jam jars

2 tablespoons vegetable oil
1kg onions, sliced
2 sprigs of thyme
3 bay leaves
75g dark brown sugar
1 teaspoon chopped thyme
   leaves
150ml balsamic vinegar
sea salt and freshly ground black
   pepper

Heat the oil in a large saucepan over a medium heat, add the sliced onions, thyme sprigs and bay leaves and cook without colouring, stirring occasionally, until soft and tender (around 30 minutes). Remove the thyme stalks and bay leaves.

Stir in the sugar, chopped thyme and balsamic vinegar, turn down the heat and very slowly dry out and caramelise for around one hour. Make sure the chutney doesn't catch on the bottom of the pan.

Place the hot mixture into sterilised jam jars (see instructions, right), seal and label.

Sterilising a jar
Fill a large pan of water, add a tablespoon of salt and bring to a rapid boil. Gently lower the preserving jars into the water, ensuring the jars are completely submerged, for around 3 minutes. Very carefully lift them out and dry in a low oven. Alternatively, they can just go through a hot cycle in the dishwasher (my preferred option for an easy life!).

Funky Herb Oil

Invest in some pretty jars for this oil – presentation is everything and really makes the difference. There are so many different flavoured oils you can make: lobster oil, chilli oil... the list is endless! In my kitchens we have many on the go, but this is a good one to get you started. Remember that garlic will ferment over time, so use this oil within a couple of weeks. Use in salads and cooking.

8 garlic cloves, peeled
2 large sprigs of rosemary
2 large sprigs of thyme
3 bay leaves
1 teaspoon black peppercorns
2 star anise
900ml olive oil

Place the garlic and all dry ingredients in a 1-litre sterilised preserving jar (see page 146). Pour the olive oil until it reaches the top, seal tightly and label.

Punchy Piccalilli

Great with any cooked cold meats – try it with my Marmalade and Honey-Glazed Ham (see page 70). This is an old-fashioned recipe. It's one that my grandma would make and it would always have a place on the table every Monday teatime, served with the cold meat from the Sunday roast and a pan of potato and veggie bubble and squeak. Using up leftovers was almost a religion back in those days, when money was sparse and you used everything and reinvented dishes.

makes approximately 3 jars

1 cauliflower, cut into small florets
200g shallots, peeled and cut half through the root
55g sea salt
600ml malt vinegar
$\frac{1}{4}$ teaspoon grated nutmeg
$\frac{1}{4}$ teaspoon ground allspice
1 small cucumber, peeled, deseeded and cut into 1cm cubes
125g green beans, topped, tailed and cut into 2.5cm lengths
$\frac{1}{2}$ red pepper, deseeded and cut into 1cm squares
80g caster sugar
1 teaspoon sea salt
1 garlic clove, crushed
$\frac{1}{2}$ tablespoon freshly grated ginger
25g English mustard powder
10g ground turmeric

15g plain flour

Place the cauliflower and shallots in a non-metallic bowl. Whisk the 55g of sea salt into 1 litre of cold water to make brine. Pour this over the vegetables, then place a plate on top to submerge them in the liquid. Leave in the fridge for 24 hours.

Drain the vegetables in a colander and gently rinse them. Place in a saucepan with the vinegar. Add the nutmeg and allspice and bring to the boil. Cover and simmer for 6–8 minutes or until the vegetables are tender.

Take off the lid and stir in the cucumber, beans, pepper, sugar, remaining teaspoon sea salt, garlic and ginger. Bring back up to the simmer and cook for 2 minutes, until the vegetables are al dente. Drain in a colander, reserving the vinegar.

Mix the mustard powder, turmeric and flour in a bowl, add a little water to make a smooth paste, then add a ladleful of the reserved hot vinegar. Stir together until smooth, then pour back into the remaining reserved vinegar and whisk thoroughly. Place the sauce back in a saucepan and bring gently back to the boil. Reduce the heat and simmer for 5 minutes, stirring occasionally.

Place the vegetables in a large bowl and pour over the hot sauce. Gently mix together.

Spoon the mixture into sterilised jars (see page 146), cover immediately with circles of waxed paper, then place the lids on.

When the jars are cold, label and store in a cool, dry, dark place. The piccalilli will be at its best if left to mature for at least a month.

Honey and Pecan Biscuit Tubes

When I make these, I tend to double or even quadruple the quantities and pop the raw 'tubes' in the freezer. Then, if you decide to visit someone on the spur of the moment, you've got a beautiful present already made, or if the outlaws turn up for coffee and a biccy unannounced, a homemade treat can be ready in minutes.

makes **10** biscuits

225g unsalted butter
75g caster sugar
1 egg yolk
1 tablespoon clear honey
250g plain flour, sifted
75g broken pecans

Cream the butter and sugar together in a bowl and add the egg yolk, honey and sifted flour to form a dough. Finally, add in the pecan nuts and stir to make sure they are evenly distributed.

Flour a work surface and roll the dough into a tube measuring roughly 5cm in diameter and 20cm in length. Wrap and roll this in baking parchment, twisting the ends so that it looks like a cracker.

Tie the 'cracker' with string and label with the following instructions: 'Slice with a hot knife into 5mm circles, place on a baking tray and bake in a preheated oven at 180°C/ Gas mark 4 for 10 minutes until golden brown.'

Chocolate-Dipped Honeycomb

You will need a sugar thermometer for this recipe, but this is a really fun recipe to make – it's almost like a science lesson when the molten honeycomb starts to froth and foam! The honeycomb looks great presented in clear Kilner-style storage jars. If you want deep big chunks of honeycomb, double the recipe and pour into a bowl lined with baking parchment; once set, the honeycomb can be broken into large shards.

serves **4–6**

100g caster sugar
4 tablespoons golden syrup
1½ teaspoons bicarbonate of soda
200g good-quality dark chocolate

Line a baking tray with baking parchment.

Mix the sugar and golden syrup to a paste in a heavy-based saucepan and slowly melt over a low-medium heat until it reaches 150°C or the hard-crack stage on a sugar thermometer.

Take the sugar off the heat and quickly beat in the bicarbonate of soda with a wooden spoon. Take care as the mixture will froth up to make honeycomb. Quickly pour the honeycomb onto the lined baking tray and allow to set at room temperature. Once set, remove the baking parchment and smash the honeycomb into shards.

Melt the chocolate in a bowl set over a saucepan of boiling water, making sure the water does not touch the bottom of the bowl. Once melted, stir the chocolate and dip the smashed-up honeycomb shards in it. Leave to set on baking parchment.

The Family Kitchen

Glittered Salted Caramel

This is an Amber production. Maximum impact with minimum input! These look and taste amazing, and as camp as you like! The caramel is great heated up and poured over good-quality vanilla ice cream. I've also featured it spooned into the bottom of my Toffee Date Pudding (see page 208).

makes **2** *jars*

240g unsalted butter
240g light muscovado sugar
200ml double cream
1–2 teaspoons sea salt
½ teaspoon edible glitter

Melt the butter and sugar together in a saucepan over a low heat. When the mixture turns golden brown, take it off the heat and very carefully whisk in the cream.

Add the salt. Taste after adding 1 teaspoon to see if it is salty enough for your taste; if not, add more. Add the glitter and allow the mixture to cool a little, then pour into sterilised jam jars (see page 146), seal and pop into the fridge to thicken.

Shortbread Stars

People can't resist shortbread, and these stars make particularly good presents for the little ones to give at Christmas as it's a nice, easy recipe for them to help with. The stars look great packed into disposable card takeaway boxes.

makes **12** *stars*

150g plain flour, plus extra for dusting
100g butter, cubed and softened
50g caster sugar, plus extra for sprinkling
2 drops vanilla extract

Put the flour into a large mixing bowl, add in the butter and rub together until the mixture resembles fine breadcrumbs. Fold in the sugar and the vanilla extract and work the mixture with your hands until it forms a ball.

Continue kneading the biscuit dough until it is smooth and the sides of the bowl are clean. Wrap the dough in clingfilm and chill in the fridge for 1 hour.

Preheat the oven to 130°C/ Gas mark ½. Line a baking tray with baking parchment.

Remove the dough from the fridge and allow to come to room temperature so that it is workable.

Lightly flour a work surface and roll out the dough until it is about 1cm thick. Using a star cutter, cut out the biscuits. Transfer these to the lined tray and bake in the preheated oven for 30 minutes until very pale gold in colour.

Remove from the oven, allow to cool a little, then sprinkle with caster sugar whilst still warm.

From left to right: Shortbread Stars (page 149); Funky Herb Oil (page 146); Glittered Salted Caramel (page 149).

Do-it-Yourself Brownie Kit

Now, I'd be chuffed if someone thought to give me this as a present! Brownies are a big hit and here you've done all the leg work by providing the bulk of the raw ingredients. Don't forget to give the actual recipe to the lucky recipient too, so that they know what to do! I like to present all the dry ingredients in a glass preserving jar.

makes **16** squares

150g chopped walnuts
125g plain flour, sifted
475g caster sugar
125g cocoa powder
1 vanilla pod

Spoon the chopped walnuts into a 1.5-litre preserving jar, then layer on the sifted flour, followed by the sugar, then finally the cocoa powder. This should create a beautiful layered effect inside the jar.

On the label write *'Add 4 eggs, 330g butter and go!'* You can then tie your label and the vanilla pod onto the clip of the preserving jar.

This is the recipe you will need to write out on paper and tuck into the jar:

Preheat the oven to 180ºC/ Gas mark 4.

Pour the brownie mix into a large bowl. Melt the butter in a saucepan over a medium heat. Once it has melted, take the saucepan off the heat and whisk into the brownie mix.

In a separate large bowl, break the eggs. Split the vanilla pod lengthways and remove the seeds. Add the seeds to the bowl and whisk gently. Pour the contents of this bowl into the one containing the brownie mix and mix together until glossy. Beat the mixture vigorously until everything is thoroughly combined.

Line a rectangular cake tin (30 x 25cm wide is perfect) with baking parchment. Pour in the cake mixture, making sure you spread it evenly across the tin. Level the top with a spatula if necessary, then bake in the preheated oven for 15–20 minutes.

Allow to cool completely before cutting.

The Family Kitchen

Malted Prune Tea Loaf

Who's for a cuppa? Time is precious, and with busy lives, we can sometimes neglect our cherished elderly members in the family. Why not make this, take it round to Nan and Grandad, listen to a few stories, share a few laughs and give them the time and love they deserve! Delicious with thickly spread butter or try with a nice wedge of vintage Lincolnshire poacher cheese.

serves **8–10**

butter, for greasing
8 tablespoons malt extract
1 tablespoon black treacle
100ml hot strong Earl Grey or English Breakfast tea (use 2 tea bags)
200g pitted prunes, cut into quarters
175g self-raising flour
1 teaspoon ground mixed spice
1 free-range egg

Preheat the oven to 140°C/ Gas mark 1. Butter a 900g loaf tin and line with baking parchment.

Mix the malt extract and treacle into the hot tea and stir until dissolved. Place the prunes in a mixing bowl, pour over the hot malt tea mixture and leave to cool.

Sift the flour and mixed spice into a large mixing bowl, add the egg and tea mixture. Stir to combine well.

Spoon into the lined loaf tin and bake for about 1–1$\frac{1}{4}$ hours. Test the loaf by piercing with a skewer – when the skewer comes out clean, the loaf is ready.

Leave to stand for 10 minutes in the tin before turning out onto a cooling rack. Once cool, wrap your loaf in baking parchment and place in an airtight container for a minimum of 2 days to mature. This loaf gets better with time.

"Why not make this, take it round to Nan and Grandad, listen to a few stories, share a few laughs and give them the time and love they deserve!"

Rhubarb, Ginger and Vanilla Pod Jam

This jam is dedicated to Grandma Kirby who spent her life making sweet beautiful jams and chutneys out of her pantry in Ruislip for the Women's Institute. It is utterly beautiful; of course, you don't have to use the very pink forced rhubarb but it really is stunning. The jam goes extremely well with scones and Jersey Cream Butter with Cornish Sea Salt (see page 154) and works as an alternative topping for the Coconut and Rhubarb Jam Bars (see page 198). Also great with roast pork. Have fun trying it with anything you like! Yum!

makes **3–4** jars

1kg forced pink rhubarb, cut into 1cm rounds
1kg jam sugar
75g fresh ginger, grated
75g Chinese stem ginger in syrup, drained and finely chopped
zest and juice of 1 unwaxed lemon
1 vanilla pod, seeds reserved

Place all the ingredients in a large heavy-based pan and stir well. Place over a high heat and bring to the boil. Continue to cook and stir rapidly for around 10–15 minutes. Use a spoon to remove any scum that appears (this will keep the jam all pretty and pink!).

To test if the jam is ready, drip a drop onto a chilled saucer – it should form a slight ripple if you drag a spoon through it. If not, boil for an additional 5 minutes and test again.

Discard the vanilla pod. While still hot, pour the jam into sterilised jars (see page 146), seal tightly and label.

Jersey Cream Butter with Cornish Sea Salt

I have to say 'big respect' to Amber who makes and packages this beautiful butter. A gift from the gods and truly amazing on hot farmhouse toast. If you can't get hold of Jersey cream, ordinary double cream will be fine. During the beating stage, around 200–300ml buttermilk will be extracted – this is perfect with Kirby Fried Buttermilk Chicken (see page 89).

serves **4**

600ml Jersey double cream
$\frac{1}{2}$ teaspoon Cornish sea salt

Pour the cream into the bowl of an electric mixer. Using the paddle or whisk, start to beat on a medium setting. After about 6 minutes the cream will look as though it is separating and will take on a yellowy cottage-cheese appearance.

Continue beating and you will see a liquid coming out – this is the buttermilk. Pour off, continue beating and keep removing the buttermilk at intervals until a butter-like consistency is achieved and no more liquid appears.

Finally, fold the sea salt into the butter. Wrap the butter in baking parchment and tie the ends. Store in the fridge.

The Family Kitchen

Seville Orange Marmalade

This marmalade is so easy to make. Any oranges will work in this recipe – I have used Seville but in February and March you should get your hands on some blood oranges. It's definitely worth trying these as they give the marmalade an amazing, beautiful pink colour. If you want to ramp it up, splash in a tablespoon of Cointreau.

*makes **6** jars*

500g Seville oranges, washed
  and dried
1/2 unwaxed lemon
1kg preserving sugar

Pour 2 litres of water into a large heavy-based saucepan. Juice the oranges and lemon, add the juice to the water and discard the lemon.

Cut the juiced oranges into quarters and, using a metal spoon, scrape the pith and seeds into the centre of a square of muslin. Tie the muslin into a bundle, to enclose the pith and seeds, and add it to the pan with the water and juice.

Cut the orange peel into thin strips (or thicker if you prefer coarse-cut marmalade) and add to the pan. Bring to the boil and simmer for 2 hours until the peel has softened and the liquid has reduced by approximately half.

Remove the muslin bag and allow the bag to cool, then squeeze all the liquid from it back into the pan. Add the sugar to the pan and stir over a low heat until all the sugar has dissolved (skim off any froth that appears).

Increase the heat and boil for 20 minutes until the mixture reaches setting point. To test, drip a drop of the marmalade onto a chilled saucer – if it has reached setting point, it should form a slight ripple if you drag a spoon through it. If not, boil for an additional 5 minutes and test again.

Stir the marmalade and pour into sterilised jars (see page 146), seal and label.

"This marmalade is so easy to make. If you want to ramp it up, splash in a tablespoon of Cointreau."

Entertaining

Oooh, these recipes were so much fun! They are ones to seriously impress your guests with!

We got all our foodie friends, chefs and family around the Kirby table to trial and test these recipes.

From our very opulent Eyes to the Sky Posh Fish Pie (page 176) to one I absolutely love, Jacob's Ladder and Guinness Cottage Pie (page 175), a comfort dish but poshed up with a Montgomery Cheddar crust and pulled rib meat throughout. Food heaven! The only trouble with all our recipe testing with friends was that the wine flowed freely and such a good time was had, we just had to do it again and again. We've had to curb it a bit now due to our expanding waistlines!

The whole of Britain goes BBQ mad the minute the sun is out. So here are some new, fresh and inspiring recipes to impress your guests – they'll definitely concur that a barbie at yours is the best and the one not to miss!

Get everyone transported from your garden to the Med with our Sea Salt and Parsley Sardine Skewers (page 162). The Beer Butt and Smoked Paprika Chicken (page 158) is a great talking point and lots of fun, and the meat is so succulent, you'll end up making this every time you want a roast chicken salad! Challenge yourself to the Vietnamese Pork

Belly and Watermelon Skewers (page 161) – these take lots of preparation but are well worth the effort. They'll be one of the best things to hit your BBQ this summer! Another favourite recipe is the Wood-Panel Rib-Eye Steak. During our recipe testing parties, we all agreed that this was the best steak we have ever eaten. There was lots of smoke and theatre – girls, you won't get to see this as the boys will be crowded round, taking notes. I can't stress enough that this is the BEST steak ever!

Finally, Amber's beautiful and sexy bites for the perfect girls' night in! Start with Mini Lobster Brioche Rolls (page 186), and for something that really will get the girls wondering at your culinary prowess, try the Spiced Lamb and Leek Cutlets (page 185), which are visually stunning and fun. Lastly, what makes this party go with a pop is the Pomegranate Fizz. I always try my luck and hold out for an invite to the girls' parties, but get sent to the local pub instead… so unfair!

I hope you enjoy these recipes as much as your friends and family will. I want them all to inspire you to party hard and enjoy the best things life has to offer! Live, eat, drink and be happy!

Beer Butt and Smoked Paprika Chicken

Bring on the summer! This is on our BBQ menu every time without fail. It's very fashionable here now, but I first saw this over 12 years ago at a food show in Chicago. The meat is so succulent from the beer steaming up inside the cavity. Use an empty spray bottle (you can get from most supermarkets) as this will be easier for basting the bird while it's cooking. If your BBQ doesn't have a lid, the chicken will take longer to cook. If the weather's not great, you can also cook it in the oven on a high heat.

serves **4**

1.5kg whole chicken
440ml can of lager or beer

For the marinade
1 tablespoon each of English mustard powder, smoked paprika, ground black pepper, sea salt, garlic powder and brown sugar
2 tablespoons maple syrup
4 tablespoons olive oil
zest and juice of 2 lemons

For the basting spray
100ml apple juice
100ml olive oil
2 tablespoons cider vinegar
1 tablespoon clear honey

Place all the marinade ingredients in a large bowl and whisk together. Place in a large clean bag. Add the chicken and seal, then massage the marinade into the chicken and leave to marinate for a minimum of 2 hours in the fridge.

Preheat your barbecue.

Put all the basting ingredients in a bowl and add half the can of lager or beer. Whisk together and pour into a clean spray bottle, shake and you're ready to go! (If you don't have a spray bottle, leave in the bowl for brushing on.)

Take the half-full can of lager or beer and place the open end in the cavity of the chicken. Carefully prop this up and balance on the preheated barbecue. Start to spray or brush on the basting and continue to do so throughout cooking. Close the lid and cook for around 50–70 minutes until the chicken reaches 70°C on a meat probe and the juices run clear when the flesh is pricked with a sharp knife.

"Bring on the summer! This is on our BBQ menu every time without fail."

Vietnamese Pork Belly and Watermelon Skewers

This is a special recipe and it's a take on a great dish from the famous Fatty Crab restaurant in New York's West Village which I've adapted so it can go on a BBQ. Believe me, make plenty as this will be the first thing to run out when feeding a crowd.

serves **4–6**

1.5kg boneless pork belly
50ml sunflower oil
$\frac{1}{2}$ watermelon, cut into 3cm cubes
8 whole blades of lemongrass
$\frac{1}{2}$ bunch of spring onions, thinly sliced
1 teaspoon pickled ginger, thinly sliced
$\frac{1}{4}$ bunch of coriander

For the marinade
3 garlic cloves
2 red chillies, deseeded
7.5cm piece of fresh ginger, peeled
$\frac{1}{2}$ bunch of spring onions
$\frac{1}{2}$ bunch of coriander
2 tablespoons sesame oil
150g dark brown sugar
100ml rice wine vinegar
200ml fish sauce
100ml light soy sauce
200ml chicken stock or water
1 star anise
1 cinnamon stick

To make the marinade, place the garlic, chilli, ginger, spring onions, coriander and sesame oil in a blender and blitz until you have a rough paste. Add the sugar, vinegar, fish sauce, soy sauce and water or stock and blitz again until all the ingredients have combined thoroughly.

Using a sharp knife, score through the pork belly skin. Place into a large bowl and pour over the marinade. Add the star anise and cinnamon stick, then cover with clingfilm and marinate in the fridge overnight or for a minimum of 4 hours.

Preheat the oven to 160°C/ Gas mark 3.

Remove the pork from the marinade (reserve the marinade) and drain on kitchen paper. Heat the sunflower oil in a frying pan and brown the pork belly on all sides until it has an even colour. Place the pork in an ovenproof casserole dish and pour over the marinade, cover with foil and place in the preheated oven. Braise gently for 2–2$\frac{1}{2}$ hours until the pork is tender.

Remove the pork from the marinade and leave to cool slightly. Line a tray with clingfilm, then place the pork belly on the tray, cover with another sheet of clingfilm and then place another flat tray on top. Weigh the pork down with a heavy dish. Place in the fridge and leave to chill overnight. Strain the remaining marinade and reserve for later.

Remove and discard the pork skin and cut the pork into 3cm cubes. Alternating the pork and melon, thread lemongrass 'skewers' with 2 or 3 pieces of each per skewer. Repeat until all pork and melon has been used.

Heat up the barbecue. Pour the reserved marinade into a saucepan and warm slightly. Brush all the skewers with the marinade, then place on the hot barbecue. Turn skewers frequently, brushing with the marinade every time, until the skewers are beautifully caramelised (this should take around 5–10 minutes).

Garnish with the thinly sliced spring onion, pickled ginger and coriander leaves.

Sea Salt and Parsley Sardine Skewers

This recipe takes me back to Spain! Sun shining, a San Miguel in hand and the aroma of these little sardines being cooked by the local fishermen. They cook these on the beach next to their boats, on skewers turned regularly over the embers. That memory has me hovering over the keyboard ready to book flights! Serve with my fresh Aioli (see page 101).

serves **4**

4 wooden skewers
12 large fresh sardines
1 teaspoon rock salt
1 teaspoon smoked paprika
2 tablespoons olive oil
2 limes, halved
$1/2$ bunch of parsley, chopped

Soak the wooden skewers in water for 1 hour (this stops them from burning during cooking).

Gut the sardines, leaving the head and tail on (or ask your fishmonger to do this for you). Season with the rock salt and smoked paprika, then drizzle with olive oil.

Heat up the barbecue.

Remove a skewer from the water and thread on the sardines widthways, 3 whole sardines per skewer. Place over a hot barbecue and turn after 2 minutes and then cook for a further 2 minutes.

Place the lime halves straight onto the barbecue to caramelise. Serve the sardine skewers sprinkled with parsley, with the caramelised limes on the side.

The Family Kitchen

Garlic, Halloumi and Fresh Rosemary Branches

I love the delicious, squeaky saltiness of halloumi. Use the main stalks of the rosemary branches as they are strong enough to support the weight of the cheese on these River Café-inspired skewers. You get an amazing flavour of rosemary permeating through.

serves **4**

8 large rosemary stalks (15–20cm long)
2 red peppers
1 large red onion
500g halloumi
2 garlic cloves, finely sliced
100ml olive oil
sea salt and freshly ground black pepper

Strip the rosemary stalks to make skewers, removing all the leaves apart from those on the top 2cm of each stalk. Soak the skewers in water for 30 minutes.

Cut the peppers in half and de-seed, then slice into 3cm squares. Cut the onion into 3cm squares. Slice the halloumi into 3cm cubes.

Thread the rosemary stalks with alternate pieces of halloumi, red onion and pepper. Place in a dish, sprinkle with the garlic and olive oil, then season. Leave to marinate in a cool place for 1 hour.

Heat up the barbecue.

Place the skewers on the hot barbecue, sear and cook for 5–10 minutes, turning regularly.

Wood-Panel Rib-Eye Steak

This is a Native American-style of cooking, where they would cook their fish and meat using wood from the local cedar trees. You can buy BBQ planks via the Internet or alternatively cut your own! Just be sure they are from untreated and natural wood, completely void of any chemicals as these could be harmful. The best woods to use are oak, cedar, cherry or beech; avoid pine as this gives a bitter taste. Have a spray bottle of water handy and keep a close eye on the BBQ plank – if it starts to flame, spray and douse with a little water. It is a little trial and error at the start, but well worth the effort! This is one of the tenderest and most succulent ways of cooking meat, and produces amazing fish too.

serves **4**

1 large plank (see introduction),
    40 x 15 x 2cm
1 litre apple juice
1 litre water
100ml Jack Daniels or any other
    whisky (optional)
4 tablespoons olive oil
4 x 150g good-quality rib-eye
    steaks
2 garlic cloves, crushed
1 tablespoon sea salt

Soak the plank in the apple juice, water and Jack Daniels, making sure it is thoroughly submerged (you may need to put a weight on it) for at least 2 hours, but ideally for as long as 6 hours.

Preheat the barbecue to a high setting. Oil one side of the plank with 1 tablespoon of olive oil and place oiled side up onto the barbecue. Close the lid and leave for 3–5 minutes for the plank to become hot.

Massage the steaks with the remaining olive oil, garlic and salt, then place on the hot plank and close the lid to bake. The plank will smoulder and smoke a lot – this all adds to the flavour so don't be tempted to keep lifting the lid as this interferes with the high temperature that is required. Leave for 6–8 minutes without opening the lid, then check on the steaks and close the lid again.

Keep an eye out for any flames and spray with the water if any appear during the cooking process. Rib-eye steaks weighing 125–150g should take around 15 minutes to cook to medium rare.

Salmon Parcels with Mussels, Star Anise and Fennel

Barbecues can tend to be a big meat fest, so we always try to show a bit of love to the less carnivorous at our BBQs – if you're not a meat eater, there's nothing worse than being shown just a jacket spud and lettuce leaf while everyone else tucks in! This is such an easy way to cook fish on the barbie, and it keeps it super-moist. If any of the mussels have not opened, discard them.

serves **4**

1 fennel bulb
6 tablespoons extra-virgin olive
 oil
2 tablespoons brown sugar
4 x 150g salmon fillets
16 mussels, cleaned and
 scrubbed
4 star anise
1 lemon, cut into 8 thin slices
½ bunch of dill, chopped
100ml white wine
sea salt and freshly ground black
 pepper

Preheat the oven to 200ºC/ Gas mark 6. Cut 4 pieces of foil measuring approximately 40 x 40cm and 4 pieces of baking parchment measuring approximately 30 x 30cm. Lay a piece of baking parchment on top of each piece of foil. Line a baking tray with baking parchment.

Cut the fennel lengthways, then slice into very thin slices around 5mm thick. Place in bowl with 2 tablespoons of olive oil and the brown sugar and stir to coat. Place on the lined baking tray and cook in the preheated oven for around 20 minutes or until caramelised. Remove from the oven to cool.

Place a salmon portion in the middle of each square of baking parchment and season. Place 4 mussels and one star anise in each parcel. Finally, divide the caramelised fennel into 4 and place on top of the salmon. Place 2 slices of lemon on top of the salmon and fennel and finish with the chopped dill. Very gently pour 25ml of the white wine over each piece of salmon (you may need to bend the foil upwards to ensure the wine doesn't run out) and finish with the remaining olive oil. Fold the foil and parchment over, then crimp and seal the parcels completely (they should look like pasties).

Place the parcels on a hot barbecue for around 15 minutes, then allow to rest for 5 minutes. Open the parcels and serve in the foil.

The Family Kitchen

Lemon and Garlic Flattened Chicken

Light up your BBQ a good hour before you're going to use it to make sure it's properly hot. This chicken is finger-licking and bone-sucking good! Prepare to get your hands dirty.

serves **4**

4 whole baby chickens (poussins)
2 tablespoons olive oil
2 lemons, halved

For the marinade
zest and juice of 2 lemons
3 sprigs of rosemary, chopped
6 sprigs of thyme, chopped
6 garlic cloves, finely chopped
2 tablespoons olive oil

1 tablespoon paprika
3 tablespoons sea salt
freshly ground black pepper

Cut through the underside of the chicken cavities with a very sharp chopping knife, then open them up and flatten out onto a chopping board.

To make the marinade, place all the ingredients in a large bowl. Place the split chickens in the marinade, then marinate in the fridge overnight or for at least 4 hours.

Heat up the barbecue. Remove the chicken from the fridge 30 minutes before cooking. Brush with olive oil and place on the barbecue skin side down. Cook carefully for about 4 minutes on each side until they are golden brown. Once you have a nice colour on both sides, move to a cooler part of the barbecue to continue cooking, making sure you turn and baste frequently with olive oil. Cook until thoroughly cooked (after around 20 minutes the juices should run clear). Place the halved lemons flesh side down on the barbecue to caramelise and serve alongside the chicken.

Rob's Perfect Rub

Oooh, er... there's potential for a few jokes here! The beauty of this rub is it goes with almost any meat, whether you fancy pork, chicken, lamb or beef. Don't limit yourself to this blend of spices – have fun making your own mixture. Store in a preserving jar and keep topped up throughout the BBQ season.

serves **4**

1 tablespoon each of soft brown sugar, garlic powder, English mustard powder, smoked paprika, cayenne pepper, freshly ground black pepper, smoked salt and chopped dried chillies

Place all ingredients in a bag and shake until thoroughly mixed together. Pour into a preserving jar and seal. Sprinkle with love over your 'fave' meat or fish.

Artichoke, Leek and Taleggio Pie

You'll need a flan ring with a diameter of 25cm for this dish. Remember to have all your ingredients ready so you can work really quickly, and keep a clean damp cloth handy to cover the filo to keep fresh and prevent it from drying out. This pie is delicious served with a heritage tomato and onion salad.

serves 6–8

2 large potatoes, peeled and chopped into 2cm cubes
$1/4$ teaspoon saffron
50g butter, for frying
50ml olive oil
2 large leeks, finely sliced and washed
2 bunches of spring onions, chopped
2 garlic cloves, finely chopped
400g tinned artichokes, drained and quartered
$1/2$ bunch of dill, chopped
juice of $1/2$ lemon
100g Parmesan cheese, grated
200g Taleggio cheese, diced into 1cm cubes
200g (about half a standard packet) filo pastry
100g butter, melted
1 teaspoon poppy seeds
1 teaspoon sesame seeds
sea salt and freshly ground black pepper

Preheat the oven to 180°C/ Gas mark 4. Line a baking tray with greased baking parchment.

Place the cubed potatoes in a saucepan, cover with water, then add the saffron and season with salt. Cook until the potatoes are tender (5–6 minutes once the water has reached boiling point), then drain thoroughly and leave to cool.

Place a very large frying pan (or 2 medium frying pans) over a medium heat and add the butter and olive oil. When the butter starts to foam, add the leeks, spring onions and garlic. Cook gently for 3–4 minutes until softened but not coloured. Remove from the heat and add the artichokes, cooked potatoes and fresh dill. Stir carefully, ensuring you don't break up the potatoes, until combined together, then squeeze over the juice of half a lemon, season and leave to cool.

Once the mixture has cooled, add the grated Parmesan and diced Taleggio cheese, season, then fold in gently.

Place a buttered 25cm flan ring on the prepared baking tray. Take a large square (around 30 x 30cm) of filo pastry and brush one side with melted butter. Lay a second square the same size over the top so that they stick together. Using a sharp knife, cut into strips 2cm wide and butter both sides again. Quickly place the end of each strip in the middle of your flan ring and fan around towards the outside, overlapping each strip, this should cover a quarter of the flan ring. Repeat the process a further 3 times to complete the circle, working quickly and then covering with a damp clean cloth to prevent the pastry from drying out. You should have around 12cm of each strip of pastry overhanging the ring – these strips will form the pastry top.

Spoon all the cheese filling gently into the pastry – there will be sufficient to overfill so pack down until it is level. Fold the pastry strips back into the middle to seal. Generously brush the top of the pie with the remaining melted butter and sprinkle over the poppy and sesame seeds. Place in the preheated oven and bake for 25–30 minutes until golden brown.

Leave to cool and rest for 15 minutes, then carefully free the pie from the sides of the ring using a small knife. Remove the ring to serve. Eat hot or cold.

Classic Coq au Vin

The story goes that Napoleon made an unexpected stop at an inn while travelling through France. The poor innkeeper had nothing in his kitchen apart from an old cock and some cheap wine, so he cooked the bird in the wine with some vegetables and to everyone's surprise and delight it was delicious and became a firm fixture of traditional French cuisine. Well, whatever happened, coq au vin really is a beautiful classic dish.

serves 4

1 whole large free-range or corn-fed chicken (around 1.5kg), cut into 8 portions, or 8 chicken thighs
6 tablespoons vegetable oil
200g button mushrooms, halved
200g shallots, peeled
6 garlic cloves, crushed and chopped
200g pancetta, cut into 1cm cubes
3 tablespoons plain flour
500ml chicken stock
20g butter
2 thick slices of white bread, cut into 1cm cubes
1 tablespoon sea salt
$\frac{1}{4}$ bunch of flat-leaf parsley, roughly chopped
salt and freshly ground black pepper

For the marinade
1 bottle medium-bodied red wine
125ml brandy
1 onion, chopped
1 large carrot, cut into 1cm rounds
1 large leek, cut into 1cm rounds
3 bay leaves
2 sprigs of fresh thyme

Place all marinade ingredients in a large bowl or large saucepan. Add the chicken portions, making sure they are submerged in the marinade. Cover with clingfilm and refrigerate for 24 hours.

Next day, strain the chicken through a colander, keeping the marinade (the liquid and the vegetables) to one side. Pour 2 tablespoons of oil into a large flameproof casserole and place over a high heat until smoking. Carefully add all the chicken, season and seal until golden brown, then carefully remove and keep to one side.

Place the casserole pan back over a high heat, add 3 tablespoons of oil, the chopped onion, carrot and leek from the marinade, and the mushrooms, shallots, garlic and pancetta. Sweat for around 5 minutes.

Stir in the flour, then add the chicken stock and remaining marinade with the thyme and bay leaves. Bring up to the boil, add the chicken, then simmer for

45 minutes until the liquid has reduced by around one-third (this should give you the correct consistency). Season to taste.

Preheat the oven to 160°C/ Gas mark 3.

Cover the casserole with a tightly fitting lid and transfer to the preheated oven. Cook slowly for 1$\frac{1}{2}$ hours.

Before serving, heat a frying pan over a medium heat, add 1 tablespoon of oil and the butter and allow to froth. Add the cubed bread and toss until golden brown, then add the sea salt and parsley. Spoon the croutons over the top of your bubbling chicken. Serve with mustard mashed potato.

The Family Kitchen

Spiced Pulled Pork and Flatbreads

This is really great with a big dollop of my Hummus (see page 34), a nice tomato, cucumber, red onion and parsley salad and these lovely warm flatbreads. Big shout to chef and friend David Steel, who has been a major support throughout the journey of this book – this is his recipe. Cheers, Dave.

serves **6–8**

2kg skinless boned pork shoulder
2 tablespoons smoked paprika
1 tablespoon ground cinnamon
1 tablespoon fresh chilli, chopped
   and deseeded
2 tablespoons sea salt
100g dark brown sugar
100ml white wine vinegar
250ml good-quality cider
2 onions, finely sliced
4 sprigs of fresh thyme
2 bay leaves
freshly ground black pepper

For the flatbread
600g strong flour
1 teaspoon sea salt
3 tablespoons baking powder
1 teaspoon ground cumin
1 teaspoon crushed fennel seeds
6 tablespoons olive oil
100ml yoghurt
200ml warm water

Place the pork in a deep casserole dish or deep roasting tin. Mix the smoked paprika, cinnamon, chilli and sea salt together, then massage into the pork.

Mix together the sugar, vinegar and cider and pour over the pork. Add the onions, thyme and bay leaves and give it all a good mix. Cover with clingfilm and marinate in the fridge overnight or for a minimum of 4 hours.

Preheat the oven to 170°C/ Gas mark 3$\frac{1}{2}$.

Remove the pork from the fridge, cover with a sheet of baking parchment and then with foil. Place in the preheated oven and cook for 4 hours, then remove the foil and parchment and cook for a further hour. Remove from the oven and leave to cool in the cooking juices.

To make the flatbread, mix flour, salt, baking powder, cumin and fennel seeds in a large mixing bowl. Using your hands, mix in the oil, yoghurt and water and work into a smooth dough (add a touch more water if the dough is too dry).

Remove the dough from the bowl onto a lightly floured work surface and knead for 5 minutes, then cover with a clean tea towel and leave the dough to rest on the side for 10 minutes. Divide the dough into 10 equal balls. Dust the work surface with more flour and roll out each ball into 15cm rounds, 5mm thick.

Cook the flatbreads in a dry frying pan for a couple of minutes on each side until the bread has puffed up and become golden. Brush with oil, then keep warm under a clean tea towel.

Remove the pork from the pan and place it on a chopping board. Using 2 forks or your hands, pull the pork apart, shredding it into small pieces. Place on a serving dish.

Strain the cooking juice through a sieve into a saucepan, then warm through gently and reduce by half. Pour just enough of the reduced cooking juices over the pork to moisten the meat and serve with the warm flatbreads.

Salmon Lasagne with Caramelised Fennel and Rocket Salad

An absolute centrepiece, like the other dishes in this chapter. This is the recipe when you want to impress, and impressed your guests will be! You will need an ovenproof dish approximately 25cm x 30cm in size. The perfect VIP lunch to serve with a crisp chilled Sauvignon.

serves **6-8**

1 litre fish stock
125g butter, plus extra for greasing
100g flour
200ml white wine
200ml double cream
zest and juice of 1 lemon
1 bunch of dill, roughly chopped
250g spinach, stalks removed
1kg fresh side of salmon fillet, skinless and boneless
6 fresh lasagne sheets (about 250g)
250g sliced smoked salmon
80g Gruyère cheese, grated
sea salt and freshly ground black pepper

For the salad
2 bulbs fennel
4 tablespoons demerara sugar
2 tablespoons olive oil
120g rocket

Preheat the oven to 180°C/Gas mark 4. Warm the fish stock in a medium saucepan.

To make the sauce, place 100g butter in a heavy-based saucepan and melt over a medium heat. Stir in the flour until a paste (roux) is formed. Cook over a gentle heat for 2 minutes without colouring, stirring continuously, then whisk in the white wine and fish stock, ensuring there are no lumps. Simmer gently for 8 minutes, stirring continuously. Remove from the heat, then whisk in the double cream, lemon zest and juice and dill. Place to one side and keep warm.

Melt the remaining 25g butter in a very large frying pan or wok over a high heat. When it starts to froth, add the spinach, turn and season with salt and pepper. Once the spinach has wilted (around 2 minutes), remove and drain in a colander, then leave to cool.

Using a sharp knife thinly slice the salmon fillet (around 5mm in thickness) along the length of the fillet. Lay the slices out on a tray and season with black pepper only.

Lightly butter a large ovenproof dish. Place a layer of fresh lasagne (2 sheets, trimmed if necessary) on the bottom, then layer with half the fresh salmon, a third of the wilted spinach and a third of the sauce.

Repeat with another layer of fresh lasagne (2 sheets), the smoked salmon, a third of the wilted spinach and a third of the sauce.

Repeat again using the remaining lasagne, fresh salmon and spinach and finally the remaining sauce. Sprinkle with grated Gruyère. Bake in the preheated oven for around 25–30 minutes until golden brown and bubbling.

To make the salad, cut the fennel in half lengthways, then, using a sharp knife, slice thinly and place in a bowl. Add the olive oil and brown sugar and mix thoroughly. Spread out evenly on a baking tray lined with baking parchment and cook in the oven for approximately 15–20 minutes until caramelised. Remove from the oven and leave to cool slightly.

Once the lasagne is ready, remove from the oven. Place the rocket in a bowl and add the baked fennel. Season with salt and black pepper, then gently toss together. Place on top of the lasagne to serve.

The Family Kitchen

Jacob's Ladder and Guinness Cottage Pie

The Family Kitchen

The pie Desperate Dan could only dream about! For this recipe, it's worth getting the short ribs if you can get hold of them; however, good-quality stewing steak will also work. This is a big recipe so allow yourself plenty of time – the result will be worth the effort. One of my personal faves, this dish needs to be attacked with lots of mates and a bottle of red. Hold back a couple of short rib bones or ask your butcher for a couple of fore rib bones for a fun garnish.

serves **6–8**

5 tablespoons vegetable oil
2kg beef short ribs or 1kg best stewing steak
4 large carrots, 2 roughly chopped and 2 cut into 1cm cubes
4 onions, 2 chopped and 2 thinly sliced
1 leek, sliced
1/2 bunch of thyme
1 teaspoon peppercorns
1 head of garlic, halved
2 bay leaves
440ml Guinness
2 litres beef stock
50ml Worcestershire sauce
1 tablespoon brown sugar
sea salt and freshly ground black pepper

For the mash
4 large Maris Piper potatoes, peeled and chopped
50g butter
100ml milk
50ml double cream
100g mature Cheddar cheese (Montgomery is perfect), grated
sea salt

Preheat the oven to 150°C/ Gas mark 2.

Pour 2 tablespoons of vegetable oil onto a large roasting tray and place over a high heat until the oil is smoking. Generously season the ribs with salt and pepper and sear and colour until golden brown, remove from the roasting tray and drain in a colander (cook these in batches to avoid crowding the pan).

Heat a further 2 tablespoons of oil in the same roasting tray, then add the roughly chopped carrots and onions, leeks, thyme, peppercorns, garlic and bay leaves. Cook for 10–12 minutes until the veg is nicely soft and browned.

Pour the Guinness into the pan and leave to reduce by half (around 5 minutes), then return the ribs to the tray and barely cover with beef stock and Worcestershire sauce. Cover with foil and place in the oven for around 4 1/2 hours, turning every hour until the meat is tender and is falling off the bone.

Carefully remove all the meat and bones from the pan and set to one side. Pass the cooking liquid through a fine sieve and pour into a clean pan, place on a medium heat and bring to the boil. Skim and reduce by half (around 20 minutes; this should give you around 750ml).

Allow the ribs to cool, then pick off all the meat, shred and chop finely into a large bowl.

Place a saucepan over a medium heat, add a tablespoon of vegetable oil and then the sliced onions, sprinkle over a tablespoon of brown sugar and caramelise for 10–15 minutes. Add in the cubed carrots and cook for a further 8 minutes until slightly softened, stirring occasionally.

Add the caramelised onions and carrots to the bowl of meat, then combine with the reduced cooking liquor. Season, then place the mixture into either individual dishes or one large dish. Leave to one side and allow to cool.

Increase the oven temperature to 190°C/Gas mark 5.

Place the chopped potatoes in a large saucepan, cover with cold water, season with salt and bring to the boil. Cook until tender, then drain thoroughly in a colander. Place back in the saucepan over a low heat, add the butter, milk and double cream and season with salt, then mash together. Place in a piping bag and pipe on top of the cottage pies (alternatively, just spoon on carefully and fluff up with a fork). Sprinkle the grated cheese over the top. Place in the oven and cook for 15–20 minutes until golden brown.

Eyes to the Sky Posh Fish Pie

There are plenty of fish pie recipes out there, but this is special. The liquor you get from the mussels lifts this dish from ordinary to extraordinary. And the lobster... well, need I say more? Just add special friends, beautiful wine and mix until thoroughly enjoyed! Alternatively, forget your friends, dim the lights and get romantic!

serves **4–6**

1 whole cooked lobster (optional)
200g raw tiger prawns
150g salmon fillet, skinned
150g natural smoked haddock, skinned
150g hake fillet, skinned
500g fresh live mussels, cleaned
200ml white wine
100g butter
2 leeks, finely sliced
1 large bulb of fennel, finely sliced
500ml fish stock
50g plain flour
300ml double cream
2 teaspoons Pommery mustard
sea salt and freshly ground black pepper

For the mashed potato
1kg floury potatoes, peeled and quartered
100ml milk
2 free-range egg yolks
50g butter

For the topping
50g fresh white breadcrumbs
50g Comté cheese, grated

If including lobster, rinse under running water, then cut off the head and tail and place to one side for the garnish. Remove all the cooked lobster meat from tail and claws and break into bite-sized pieces if necessary. Cut the tiger prawns in half lengthways and remove the black vein. Dice the salmon, haddock and hake into 4cm cubes.

Heat a saucepan, add the mussels and white wine, cover with a lid and place over a high heat. Shake the pan every now and then to cook the mussels until they open (around 2 minutes). Drain and reserve the cooking liquor (you will need this for the sauce).

Allow the mussels to cool for 5 minutes, then remove the meat from the shells, disposing of any unopened mussels.

Melt half the butter in a large saucepan, add the sliced leeks and fennel and cook gently without colouring for 3 minutes, then add the fish stock and bring to a simmer. Add the salmon, haddock and hake and simmer for a further 2 minutes only.

Gently remove all the fish, leeks and fennel from the pan with a slotted spoon and place in a pie dish. Add the raw prawns, cooked mussels and lobster meat. Leave the remaining fish stock simmering in the pan.

Strain the reserved cooking liquor from the mussels through a fine sieve into the fish stock.

To make the sauce, melt the remaining butter in a pan over a medium heat, stir in the flour and cook for a further 2 minutes. Gradually whisk the hot fish stock into the pan to thicken and cook for a further 5 minutes. Season to taste, then whisk in the cream and mustard, ensuring there are no lumps. Remove from the heat and leave to cool for 30 minutes.

Preheat the oven to 180°C/ Gas mark 4.

Whilst the sauce is cooling, place the potatoes in a large pan of salted water, bring to the boil and simmer for 15 minutes or until cooked through. Drain in a colander, then return the potatoes to the pan and mash. Mix in the milk, egg yolks and butter and season.

Pour the cooled sauce into the pie dish, making sure it just covers the fish completely (keep any remaining sauce to one side, then gently reheat and serve with the pie). Top with the mashed potato and bake in the oven for 20 minutes, then sprinkle the top with breadcrumbs and cheese and return to the oven for a further 10 minutes until bubbling and golden brown on top. Garnish with the lobster head and tail for 'eyes to the sky'.

The Family Kitchen

Roast cod, Minestrone Spring Vegetables and Crispy Parma Ham

A very clean dish – the flavours of minestrone really complement the beautiful white sweet flesh of the cod. Finishing the dish with a salty Parma ham crisp gives it a modern bistro edge.

serves **4**

2 tablespoons olive oil
1 onion, finely chopped
2 garlic cloves, crushed and
    chopped
100g pancetta, diced into 1cm
    cubes
1 leek, cut in half lengthways and
    then into 1cm slices
1 large carrot, cut into 1cm cubes
1 courgette, cut into 1cm cubes
$1/4$ savoy cabbage, cut into 1cm
    strips
2 tins of chopped tomatoes
200ml tomato juice
100g spaghetti
$1/2$ bunch of basil, finely chopped
4 x 150g cod fillets
4 slices Parma ham
20g Parmesan cheese, grated
sea salt and freshly ground black
    pepper

For the crust
100g butter
100g breadcrumbs
$1/2$ bunch of parsley, chopped

Heat the oil in a large saucepan over a medium heat, add the onion and garlic and fry without colouring until soft (around 3 minutes). Then turn up the heat, add the pancetta, leek and carrot and fry until crispy, stirring and shaking the pan, for around 4–5 minutes. Finally add the courgette and cabbage and fry for a further 5 minutes until soft. Turn down the heat and add the chopped tomatoes and tomato juice. Gently bring up to a slow boil, then simmer for a further 5–8 minutes.

Place the spaghetti into a saucepan of boiling water and cook until tender (around 10 minutes). Refresh under cold running water, drain well, then chop into 5cm lengths. Gently fold into your minestrone sauce, season to taste, add the basil and keep warm.

Preheat the oven to 180°C/ Gas mark 4.

For the crust, place the butter in a saucepan and slowly melt, then add the breadcrumbs and chopped parsley, stir together and season. Remove from the heat and allow to cool.

Pack the breadcrumbs firmly on the top of the cod pieces to make the crust. Place the cod on an oiled and baking-parchment-lined baking tray and bake in the preheated oven for 8–10 minutes. Once cooked, the fish should be firm to touch (if you have a probe, this should read 65°C plus).

Preheat the grill. Place the slices of Parma ham under the hot grill until crispy on both sides (2 minutes each side).

Divide the chunky minestrone into 4 bowls and place the cod on top. Finish with a glug of olive oil, a sprinkling of Parmesan and the crispy Parma ham.

The Family Kitchen

Caraway and Fennel Crispy Pork Belly with Patatas Bravas

I love this dish! The pork belly is amazing with its salty crackling and works really well with the smoky patatas bravas. Often eaten with our good friends in the beautiful mountainous Mijas in Spain, washed down with a quality Rioja while the sun sets. Perfect!

serves **4**

1 tablespoon fennel seeds
1 tablespoon caraway seeds
2 tablespoons sea salt
6 garlic cloves, chopped
6 tablespoons olive oil
1.5kg free-range pork belly, skin on and scored
2 carrots, roughly chopped
1 large onion, roughly chopped
½ bunch of celery, roughly chopped

For the patatas bravas
2 tablespoons olive oil
1 onion, finely chopped
2 garlic cloves, chopped
1 tin of chopped tomatoes
4 large potatoes, peeled and diced into 1cm cubes
vegetable oil, for frying
1 teaspoon smoked paprika
200ml crème fraîche
½ bunch of flat-leaf parsley
sea salt and freshly ground black pepper

Place the fennel seeds, caraway seeds, sea salt, garlic and 4 tablespoons of olive oil in a mortar and pound to a purée with the pestle (the seeds will remain whole but will be bruised to release their flavour). Rub and massage this mixture thoroughly into the pork skin, then marinate for 1–2 hours at room temperature.

Preheat the oven to 220°C/Gas mark 7.

Pour 2 tablespoons of olive oil onto a large roasting tray and place in the oven until hot (around 5 minutes). Carefully place the pork skin side up in the hot roasting tray, place in the oven and crisp the skin for 30–45 minutes.

Once crispy, remove the pork from the roasting tray and put to one side. Place the chopped carrots, onion and celery in the roasting tray, then place the pork skin side up over the top. Turn the oven down to 160°C/Gas mark 3 and slow cook for a further 2 hours, then remove from the oven and leave to rest for 30 minutes.

To make the patatas bravas, place 2 tablespoons of oil in a saucepan, add the onion and garlic and soften without colouring over a low heat for around 3 minutes. Add the chopped tomatoes and bring to the boil. Once boiling, turn down to a very low heat and simmer for 5–7 minutes, then season. Keep warm.

Wash the potato cubes and pat dry on kitchen paper. Plug in your deep-fat fryer or place enough vegetable oil in a deep saucepan and heat to approximately 170°C. Fry the potatoes for 3–4 minutes until crisp and golden brown, then season and dust with a teaspoon of smoked paprika and drain on kitchen paper.

Place your potatoes in a serving dish, pour over your chopped tomatoes and finish with crème fraîche and flat-leaf parsley. Serve next to your crispy pork.

Pomegranate Fizz

The ruby red of the pomegranate mixed with a good Prosecco is a great combo! It's really a thing of beauty to behold. This makes a great Christmas cocktail and slips down a treat.

serves **8**

1 bottle Prosecco
100ml pomegranate juice
1 pomegranate, seeded
4 teaspoons amber sugar crystals
80ml good-quality brandy

Open the Prosecco and pour carefully into a large jug.
Add the pomegranate juice.

Put $\frac{1}{2}$ teaspoon of pomegranate seeds into 8 large champagne flutes, followed by $\frac{1}{2}$ teaspoon of amber sugar crystals.
Add 2 teaspoons of brandy to each glass and finally top with the Prosecco and pomegranate.
Enjoy!

"This makes a great Christmas cocktail and slips down a treat."

Breaded Padron Peppers Stuffed with Goat's Cheese

A wonderful nibble – people just can't leave them alone! Padron peppers are also great fried simply in a little olive oil and salt. Very tasty, but be careful – one in every 30 packs a fiery punch! Who's for a game of Padron roulette? When selecting the peppers, try to get the largest ones possible as they are easier to stuff. If you have any goat's cheese left, you can use it for the Tomato and Goat's Cheese Tart (see page 124).

serves 4

1 bag Padron peppers (130g)
100g soft goat's cheese log, at room temperature
150ml double cream
3 free-range eggs
50g flour
100g panko breadcrumbs
vegetable oil, for frying
sea salt
crème fraîche, to serve

Carefully remove the top, stalk and white core of each pepper using a sharp knife, ensuring that you make a hole large enough to pipe the goat's cheese through. Tap each pepper to remove all the seeds – you may need to use a sharp knife.

Place the goat's cheese in a mixing bowl and mash with a fork. Whisk and beat in the double cream until you get a soft ice-cream texture (this can be done in a food processor).

Place the goat's cheese mixture in a piping bag fitted with a small straight nozzle, or use a disposable piping bag and snip a small hole in the end. Carefully pipe and fill the inside of each padron pepper, then place them in the fridge for 20 minutes to chill.

Whisk the eggs in a bowl. Place the flour and breadcrumbs in 2 separate bowls. Dip the peppers first in the flour, then in the egg and finally in the breadcrumbs. Do this twice for a really crispy coating.

Plug in the deep-fat fryer or place enough vegetable oil in a deep saucepan and heat to approximately 170°C. Using a slotted spoon or the fryer basket, gently place the breadcrumbed peppers into the fryer and fry for 2–3 minutes until golden brown. Remove and drain on kitchen paper, then season with sea salt.

Allow to rest for 5–10 minutes as they are red-hot! Serve piled high with a crème fraîche dip.

Spiced Lamb and Leek Cutlets

This is a very cool party piece! The leeks threaded through the 'eye' of the lamb look stunning – all your guests will be impressed and want to know how you did it! My nod to Wales and all its lovely produce.

serves **4**

4 x 3-bone racks of lamb, French trimmed
2 leeks
1 tablespoon olive oil, plus extra for oiling the leeks
1 teaspoon each of marjoram, oregano, cumin, chilli powder and sea salt
2 tablespoons seeded mustard
sea salt and freshly ground black pepper

Preheat the oven to 180ºC/ Gas mark 4.

Take one of the racks of lamb and carefully push the point of a sharp knife through the middle of the eye of the meat. Take a sharpening steel and thread it through, making a hole all the way through the meat. You then need to increase the size of the hole to match the width of the leek – you can do this by rolling the lamb on the steel or getting stuck in with your hands, using your fingers to stretch the meat (or try the neck of a wine bottle which is just about the right diameter). Repeat with the remaining racks of lamb.

Cut 2 whole leeks in half to make 4 pieces measuring 10cm in length and 1.5–2cm in diameter. Place in seasoned boiling water and blanch for exactly 2 minutes. Rinse in a colander under cold running water and pat dry with kitchen paper. Oil the leek all over and season with salt and pepper. Gently push this through the hole in the lamb.

Shake all the dry ingredients together in a bag. Spread the seeded mustard over the top of each rack, then dust with the spicy dry mix.

Place an ovenproof frying pan over a high heat, add 1 tablespoon of olive oil and allow to smoke, then sear the leek-studded lamb on both sides to a golden brown. Transfer to the preheated oven and cook for around 20–30 minutes (if using a meat probe, the temperature should reach 55ºC).

To serve, trim the leeks level either side of the rack of lamb and then slice into cutlets.

"This is a very cool party piece! ...all your guests will be impressed and want to know how you did it!"

Scallop and Pancetta Lollipops

A very sophisticated and adult lollipop! These went down a storm when I made them at a cooking demo for the opening of Waitrose in John Lewis's food hall at Bluewater shopping mall. They're not hard to make and are delicious. Serve in a large glass or jam jar.

serves **4**

8 x 15cm wooden bamboo
    skewers
8 large scallops, without the coral
8 thin slices of pancetta
2 tablespoons olive oil
1 lemon
freshly ground black pepper

Soak the skewers in cold water for at least 30 minutes before using.

Preheat the oven to 180°C/ Gas mark 4. Line a baking tray with baking parchment.

Make sure the scallops are nice and clean with the orange roe removed, then season on both sides with black pepper. Wrap a piece of pancetta around the outside of each scallop and insert skewers where the pancetta overlaps to prevent it from unravelling during cooking.

Preheat a large frying pan over a high heat. Add the olive oil to the pan; when it starts smoking, carefully add the scallops and seal on both sides. When all the scallops are golden brown, transfer to the lined baking tray and place in the oven for 2–3 minutes just to crisp up the pancetta.

Remove from the oven and generously squeeze over the lemon juice. Serve hot.

Mini Lobster Brioche Rolls

Amber loves serving these with plenty of Prosecco! The wasabi gives it gentle sophisticated warmth, although you could use dill or a simple lemon mayo. Just add cocktails and the girls, and let the good times roll!

serves **4**

250g cooked lobster meat,
    chopped
5 tablespoons mayonnaise
$1/4$ teaspoon wasabi
1 teaspoon chopped fresh
    tarragon
juice of 1 lime
10 mini brioche rolls (or bridge
    rolls)
sea salt and freshly ground black
    pepper

Place the chopped lobster meat in a bowl, fold in the mayonnaise, wasabi and tarragon, then squeeze in the lime juice and season. Split the brioche or bridge rolls down the middle and fill.

Serve with a glass of fizz and smiles all round!

The Family Kitchen

Mini Smoked Chicken Caesar Salad

This is so quick and easy, leaving you plenty of time to get yourself glammed up before guests arrive!

serves **4**

2 Little Gem lettuce
2 cooked smoked chicken breasts, chopped into 5mm cubes
2 tablespoons mayonnaise
2 tablespoons olive oil
2 slices of white bread, cut into 1cm cubes
25g Parmesan cheese, finely grated
$1/4$ bunch of flat-leaf parsley, chopped
sea salt and freshly ground black pepper

Preheat the oven to 180°C/ Gas mark 4. Line a baking tray with baking parchment.

Remove the roots from the lettuces and break them into individual leaves, wash and pat dry. You will need 8–12 whole leaves.

Place the chicken in a bowl, add the mayonnaise, stir and season, then place to one side.

Place a frying pan over a medium heat, add the oil and warm until smoking, then add the cubed bread and fry until golden brown. Season and drain on kitchen paper.

To make the Parmesan crisps, sprinkle tablespoon-sized mounds of grated Parmesan on the lined baking tray and flatten into circles 5cm in diameter. Place in the preheated oven for 10 minutes until melted and golden brown. Remove and allow to cool and crisp up.

Take a lettuce leaf and spoon the smoked chicken mixture into the centre, top with croutons and Parmesan crisps, and finish with some parsley.

Entwined Anchovies

The perfect Spanish romance! I was introduced to this combination of ingredients by a lovely man named Rudi from Spanish food supplier Brindisa. It was one of the nicest tasting experiences – Fresh and salty, all in one mouthful. I have topped the anchovies off with Andalucian Manzanilla olives. Enjoy this simple, uncomplicated romance!

makes **12** *skewers*

50g fresh anchovies, marinated in oil and vinegar, drained
50g jar or tin of salted anchovies
50g pitted Manzanilla olives

Entwine the anchovies together on a wooden cocktail stick – one fresh and one salted together. Top with a stoned olive. It's really that simple! Perfect for drinks.

The Family Kitchen

Butterflied Coconut Prawns

Another lovely Thai dish often sold as inexpensive street food. Thais tend to eat on the street a lot and if they want to take food away with them, it is put in clear little bags, ready for eating later on. Although Thais generally drizzle sweet chilli sauce on these prawns, my version is served with a nice mango mayo. I have also served a refreshing lime mayo which works very well too.

serves **4**

20 peeled tiger prawns
2 free-range eggs
75g plain flour
125g fresh breadcrumbs
50g desiccated coconut
4 tablespoons spicy mango chutney
4 tablespoons mayonnaise
vegetable oil, for frying
2 limes, cut into wedges
sea salt and freshly ground black pepper

Lay the prawns flat on a chopping board and carefully run a sharp knife along the inside (belly side) of each prawn, from the head to the tip of the tail. Cut into the flesh to around three-quarters of the way through and gently press open to butterfly.

Whisk the eggs in a bowl, sift the flour into a separate bowl and combine the breadcrumbs and coconut in a third bowl, so you now have 3 bowls in front of you. Dip the prawns first in the flour, then in the egg and finally in the breadcrumbs and coconut, then repeat with each prawn for a really crispy coating.

Stir the mango chutney into the mayonnaise and season.

Heat up the deep-fat fryer or place enough vegetable oil in a deep saucepan and heat to approximately 180°C. Gently lower the prawns into the hot oil using a slotted spoon or the fryer basket and cook for 2–3 minutes until golden brown.

Drain on kitchen paper and serve with lime wedges and mango mayo.

"A lovely Thai dish often sold as inexpensive street food... served with a nice mango mayo."

The Family Bakery

If you want to get your brood into the art of cooking then start them on this sweet and sticky section!

Some might say this is the yummiest chapter in the book. Who am I to disagree with them?! Try the retro 1970s Mars Bar Salted Tray Crunch (page 196) – this is so easy and only lasts about 10 minutes in our chocolate-loving home. If you want to impress, invite a loved one round for afternoon tea and a Mini Vicky Kiss (page 194).

For a reunion with your childhood, try our Damson and Blackberry Plate Pie (page 207), inspired by my grandfather's love of growing and my grandmother's passion for home baking. Lastly, the sweetshop is all a family fave, featuring the lovely Imani's Jaw-sticking Peanut Butter Fudge (page 212). Or another retro classic is my Coconut Ice (page 215), which also makes great presents. Have a go at Willy Wonka's Chocolate Box (page 210), great for parties – children or adults, we're all just big kids really! The main thing is to get in the kitchen together with the kids and have fun making and baking. Set them on the right road by teaching them and giving them the gift of being able to cook. The pleasure on their faces when they've made something tasty that they can eat is worth a few broken eggs and flour spillages on the floor.

Salted Caramel Shortbread Hearts

So easy to make, these are very beautiful little shortbread kisses. If you don't have a heart-shaped cutter, feel free to use any shape. Amber makes these for gifts to our friends – they mean so much as they are made with love from the heart!

makes **6**

100g butter, cubed and softened
150g plain flour, sifted
50g caster sugar
2 drops vanilla extract
icing sugar, for dusting

For the salted caramel
120g unsalted butter
120g light muscovado sugar
100ml double cream
1 teaspoon rock salt

Rub the butter into the flour until it resembles fine breadcrumbs, then fold in the sugar and vanilla extract. Work the mixture until it forms a smooth ball and leaves the sides of the bowl clean. Cover the dough with clingfilm and refrigerate for 1 hour.

Preheat the oven to 140°C/ Gas mark 1. Line a baking tray with a sheet of baking parchment.

Remove the dough from the fridge and allow to come up to room temperature. Lightly flour a work surface and roll the dough out until it is 1cm thick. Using a heart-shaped cutter, cut out 12 hearts and place on the lined baking tray. Bake for 30 minutes or until they are very pale gold in colour. Using a spatula or fish slice, carefully transfer to a wire cooling rack.

To make the salted caramel, melt the butter and sugar in a pan over a low heat, shaking the pan gently from time to time. Once the mixture is golden brown and frothing, remove from the heat and whisk in the double cream. Stir in the salt, leave to cool and then pop it in the fridge for 1–2 hours to thicken.

Once the biscuits and caramel have cooled, assemble by covering one biscuit with a layer of the salted caramel and placing another biscuit on top.

Serve by dusting each biscuit with icing sugar for a fairytale look.

"Amber makes these for gifts to our friends ...made with love from the heart!"

The Family Kitchen

Mini Vicky Kisses

Simple, honest and timeless, these are really beautiful mini Victoria sponges – great for afternoon tea. You can buy specially designed small, straight-sided tray moulds for these from renowned quality kitchen shops. These are always a joy to make and are a great way to learn basic sponge recipes before going on to the big league of baking!

makes **12**

225g unsalted butter, softened
225g caster sugar
4 large free-range eggs
1/2 teaspoon vanilla extract
225g self-raising flour
100g good-quality strawberry jam

For the buttercream
150g unsalted butter
300g icing sugar, plus extra for
   dusting
1/2 teaspoon vanilla extract

Preheat the oven to 180°C/ Gas mark 4. Grease the moulds and dust with flour.

Put the butter into a mixing bowl and beat with a wooden spoon until pale and creamy. Gradually fold in the sugar and beat until light and fluffy.

Crack the eggs into a small bowl and whisk together, then whisk in the vanilla extract. Very slowly add the eggs and vanilla mixture to the butter and sugar, a tablespoon at a time. Scrape down the sides of the bowl and beat in completely. Sift the self-raising flour onto the batter, stopping frequently to ensure you fold it in thoroughly.

Divide the batter between the mini cake moulds, filling them three-quarters of the way up, then smooth the tops with the back of a warm teaspoon.

Bake on the middle shelf of the preheated oven for around 15 minutes until golden brown and risen – check by inserting a wooden skewer; if it comes out clean, the cakes are ready. Allow to rest for a few minutes, then remove from the moulds and place on a cooling rack.

To make the buttercream, cream the butter, sugar and vanilla extract together until pale and glossy.

Carefully cut each cake in half. Spread the cut side of the bottom with the buttercream and the cut side of the top with a spoon of jam, then sandwich together. Dust the tops with icing sugar.

"These are always a joy to make and are a great way to learn basic sponge recipes before going on to the big league of baking!"

The Family Kitchen

Tabitha's Glitter-Bombed Rice Krispie Cakes

These cakes sparkle and are one of Tab's favourites – colourful, fun, sweet and gorgeous, just like her. Only a dad can say that!

makes **16–20** *squares*

60g butter
300g mini marshmallows
200g Rice Krispies
2 x 35g bags of white or milk
   Maltesers
$1/2$ teaspoon each of edible gold
   and edible silver

Line a 30 x 20 x 3cm baking tin with baking parchment, overlapping the edges.

Gently melt the butter in a saucepan over a low heat, add the marshmallows and stir continuously until melted and smooth (around 3 minutes).

Place the Rice Krispies in a large mixing bowl and fold in the melted marshmallows.

Spoon the mixture into the lined baking tin and pack down with slightly wet hands. Finally, push in the Maltesers and sprinkle with the edible gold and silver for a fun look.

Allow to cool and set, then remove from the tin and cut into squares or bars.

"...colourful, fun, sweet and gorgeous..."

Mars Bar Salted Tray Crunch

My auntie used to make these beauties, and I used to chomp on them as a child. They are straight out of the 1970s – a time when everybody in England was holding fondue parties and spaghetti bolognese was the dinner party special! Wow, how we've moved on with food! However, these bad boys still stand up today and don't stay in the fridge for very long!

makes **16–20** squares

4 Mars Bars, chopped very small
3 tablespoons golden syrup
1 teaspoon coarse sea salt
100g unsalted butter
150g Rice Krispies
150g dark chocolate, chopped

Line a 30 x 20 x 3cm baking tin with baking parchment.

Place the Mars Bars, golden syrup, salt and butter in a bowl set over a pan of boiling water, making sure the water doesn't get into the mixture. Bring the water up to a simmer and slowly melt the mixture, stirring occasionally, until all the ingredients are combined and glossy with a thick, smooth texture (around 8–10 minutes).

Remove the bowl from the saucepan and fold in the Rice Krispies. Pour the mixture into the lined baking tin and pack down evenly. Chill in the fridge for 30 minutes.

Place the chocolate in a bowl and carefully microwave, or melt in a bowl set over a pan of boiling water.

Remove the cake from the tin and cut into squares. Place the squares on a cooling rack and drizzle or pipe the melted chocolate over the top.

"...straight out of the 1970s... these bad boys still stand up today and don't stay in the fridge for very long!"

White Chocolate Blondies

A fab favourite with all! The raspberry tartness cuts through the sweet chocolate, making these a great traybake for any occasion. When adding the raspberries, fold them in very gently, as they will break up, although a few crushed ones look natural and beautiful.

makes **20** *squares*

230g butter
240g good-quality white
 chocolate, chopped
2 free-range eggs, beaten
340g soft brown sugar
1 vanilla pod, seeds reserved
280g plain flour
pinch of sea salt
2 teaspoons baking powder
100g fresh raspberries

Preheat the oven to 180°C/ Gas mark 4. Lightly butter a 30 x 20 x 3cm tin and line with baking parchment.

Put the chocolate and butter in a large heatproof bowl and place over a pan of simmering water, making sure the water doesn't get into the mixture. Stir until the mixture is melted and smooth. Remove from the heat and leave to cool slightly.

Whisk the eggs, sugar and vanilla seeds together in a bowl. Carefully fold in the cooled melted chocolate until thoroughly mixed and creamy. Sift in the flour, salt and baking powder and fold in gently, keeping the mixture light and fluffy. Stir in the raspberries, then pour gently into the lined tin.

Bake in the preheated oven for 30–40 minutes. When baked, the top should be crispy and the inside should still be moist.

Transfer the cake to a cooling rack and leave to cool. Cut into squares and serve.

Coconut and Rhubarb Jam Bars

Here I've used Grandma Kirby's Rhubarb, Ginger and Vanilla Pod Jam (see page 154). You can use any jam, but generally raspberry jam takes number-one slot. Passion fruit would also make a sublime marriage of flavours. Make sure you use half-fat coconut milk as this will give your sponge flavour but is not too heavy.

makes **12-16** bars

150ml half-fat coconut milk
70g desiccated coconut
225g unsalted butter
225g caster sugar
$\frac{1}{2}$ teaspoon vanilla extract
4 large free-range eggs
225g self-raising flour
$\frac{1}{2}$ teaspoon baking powder
200g rhubarb jam

Preheat the oven to 180°C/ Gas mark 4. Line a 30 x 20 x 3cm baking tin with baking parchment.

In a saucepan, heat up the coconut milk and 50g desiccated coconut, bring to the boil, remove from the hob and allow to cool.

Place all the butter, sugar, vanilla extract, eggs, flour and baking powder in a blender with the cooled coconut milk mixture and blitz until smooth. Pour into the lined baking tin and bake in the preheated oven for 25–30 minutes until golden brown. Check the cake is cooked by inserting a wooden skewer into the centre – if it comes out clean, then the cake is ready. Remove from the oven and allow to cool in the tin.

Gently warm the rhubarb jam in a small saucepan over a low heat, then brush over the top of the sponge and sprinkle with the remaining desiccated coconut.

Cointreau and Orange Marmalade Roly Poly

Mmm, a firm winter-warmer favourite. This is another classic from the Kirby family food tree that will always have a place in our hearts. I've added a splash of Cointreau, which my grandparents wouldn't have heard of or entertained! Bring on the custard and clotted cream and skip the scales for a while!

serves **8**

250g self-raising flour
200g caster sugar
25g butter, softened
125g vegetarian suet
zest of 1 orange
150ml milk
1 free-range egg yolk
200g good-quality marmalade, or use the recipe on page 155
25ml Cointreau

Preheat the oven to 170°C/ Gas mark 3½.

Place a deep roasting tin in the bottom of the preheated oven and half-fill with hot water – this creates a water bath to steam while the roly poly cooks.

Sift the flour into a large bowl, add the sugar and butter and, using your fingertips, work the butter into the flour until crumbly. Add the suet and orange zest and mix in well. Make a well in the centre and add the milk and egg yolk. Using your hands, mix together until you have a sticky dough.

Spoon the marmalade into a bowl, add the Cointreau and mix together. Reserve 4 tablespoons of the marmalade in a small saucepan for glazing.

Lightly flour the work surface and roll out the dough into a rectangle measuring 20 x 25cm and around 1cm thick. Spread with the marmalade, leaving a 2cm gap around the edges, then roll the dough up along the longer edge to make a Swiss-roll shape.

Butter a piece of baking parchment slightly larger than the roll, then wrap loosely around the roll. Now wrap the whole roll in foil, but not too tightly as the roll will expand during cooking. Place straight on the preheated oven rack, above the steaming water bath. Cook for 45–50 minutes.

Remove the roll from the oven and leave to cool in the wrapping for a couple of minutes. Gently warm the remaining Cointreau and marmalade mixture over a medium heat. Remove the roly poly from the wrapping and place on a serving dish, then glaze generously with the Cointreau and marmalade mixture.

The Family Kitchen

Gin Bramble Jelly

Gin brambles are bang on trend in all of London's cocktail bars. I've turned this into a jelly which is light and really refreshing. If you can't get blackberry liquer then Chambord is just as good. Be cautious with the lemon juice, as too much will stop it from setting.

serves **4**

5 leaves of gelatine
120ml gin
100ml blackberry liqueur or
    Chambord
500ml soda water
150g caster sugar
$\frac{1}{2}$ teaspoon lemon juice
200g blackberries
200ml double cream
1 lemon, cut into wedges,
    to garnish

Soak the gelatine in cold water.

Gently warm the gin, blackberry liqueur, soda water and sugar in a saucepan over a low heat. Using your hands, squeeze out any water from the gelatine, then slowly stir the gelatine into the saucepan until completely dissolved. Pour in the juice of the lemon and allow to simmer and clear for another 2 minutes. Skim the top, pour into a jug and allow to cool.

Divide the blackberries between 4 glass tumblers, reserving 4 berries for the garnish, then pour on the gin bramble and place in the fridge to set.

Whisk the double cream and place into a piping bag fitted with a star nozzle. Pipe a rosette of cream on top of each jelly and finish with a lemon wedge and a fresh blackberry.

"I've turned this into a jelly which is light and really refreshing."

Banging Banoffee and Pecan Shots

Mmmm... what can I say about these? They won't win you any friends at the slimming club! Enjoy the naughtiness, and we won't tell if you won't!

makes **4** *large or* **10** *shots*

397g tin of condensed milk
100g butter
150g caster sugar
2 teaspoons water
100g pecan nuts
80g digestive biscuits, crushed
50g granulated brown sugar
2 large ripe bananas, sliced
250ml double cream
125g mascarpone cheese
2 Crunchie bars

To make the toffee, boil the sealed tin of condensed milk in a large pan of water for 2–2½ hours, ensuring the tin is always covered in water. Carefully remove and allow to cool.

Melt half the butter, the caster sugar and the water in a heavy-based saucepan over a medium heat and shake gently until it begins to bubble and caramelise to a golden brown. Add the pecan nuts and mix them in, making sure they are well coated. Tip onto baking parchment and allow to cool.

Crush the digestive biscuits in a bowl. Melt the remaining butter, then pour over the biscuits and stir in the brown sugar. Spoon into the bottom of the serving glasses or shot glasses and place in the fridge.

Once set, open the tin of cooled condensed milk and spoon the toffee over the biscuit base. Layer the sliced banana on top.

Semi-whip the double cream, gently fold in the mascarpone and spoon over the top of the banana to just below the top of the glass.

Break the Crunchie bars into shards and push into the cream. Top with the caramelised pecans.

Pimm's Preserving-Jar Trifle

Pimm's originated in an oyster bar in the city of London in 1840, when James Pimm created a house cup with liqueurs and fruit extract. Perfect for summer, I used to make these for Wimbledon picnic hampers. You can make your custard, but there are a lot of quality ready-made ones out there.

serves **4**

2 leaves of gelatine
100ml lemonade
60ml Pimm's
25ml vodka
50g caster sugar
50g amaretti biscuits
250g punnet strawberries, quartered (keep 4 whole for garnish)

For the topping
400g good-quality ready-made thick custard
150ml double cream
$\frac{1}{4}$ cucumber, sliced, for garnish
4 large whole strawberries, to garnish
4 mint tops, to garnish

Soak the gelatine leaves in cold water. Place the lemonade, Pimm's, vodka and caster sugar in a saucepan and gently warm. Using your hands, squeeze out any water from the gelatine, then stir the gelatine into the saucepan and melt into the mix. Pour into a jug and allow to cool.

Crush the amaretti biscuits into pieces. Place the broken biscuits in 4 200ml Kilner jars and divide the chopped strawberries between the jars. Pour the Pimm's jelly into the jars until they are around half full. Place in the fridge and allow to set for 1–2 hours.

Once set, remove from the fridge and spoon 2 tablespoons of custard into each jar. Semi-whip the cream, then spoon this over the custard. Serve garnished with sliced cucumber, a whole strawberry and the mint tops.

"Perfect for summer, I used to make these for Wimbledon picnic hampers."

Damson and Blackberry Plate Pie

This takes me straight back to my childhood. We shared a big Victorian house in London with my grandparents. There was a lot of land attached to the house so my grandfather and dad grew everything together. My nan would deal with various seasonal soft fruit as it came into season. My grandparents' loving relationship was an inspiration. In the late afternoons, my nan would hang a tea towel at the kitchen window to indicate that dinner was ready. My grandfather would pick a flower and take it in to her every day – that's real love and a wonderful memory. Now go and bake that pie...

serves **6**

For the pastry
230g plain flour
80g icing sugar
pinch of sea salt
1 teaspoon thyme leaves
120g butter, softened, plus extra for greasing
1 free-range egg, beaten
cold water

For the filling
160g blackberries
650g damsons, stones removed and cut into quarters (use plums if damsons are not available)
100g caster sugar
30g white breadcrumbs
1 vanilla pod, seeds reserved
3 tablespoons cornflour
pinch of cinnamon

For the glaze
1 egg yolk
1 teaspoon caster sugar

To make the pastry, place the flour, icing sugar, salt and thyme in a mixing bowl. Dice the softened butter and add to the flour, gently using your fingertips to work the butter and flour together to make a crumbly mixture. Gradually add in the beaten egg and work gently until the pastry comes together (you may need to add a drop of water; if the pastry looks dry, do not knead or overwork). Wrap the pastry in clingfilm and place in the fridge to rest for about an hour.

Preheat the oven to 180°C/ Gas mark 4. Lightly butter a 30cm ovenproof plate.

Remove the pastry from the fridge 10 minutes before you need to roll it. Lightly flour a work surface and roll out the pastry to a thickness of 5mm and large enough to cut out 2 circles 2–3cm bigger than the plate. Line the plate with one piece of the pastry, then place back into the fridge to rest, along with the other piece of pastry.

Mix the blackberries, damsons, sugar, breadcrumbs, vanilla seeds, cornflour and cinnamon in a bowl. Pile the fruit into the middle of the pastry-lined plate, place the other piece of pastry carefully over the top, then crimp all around the edges to seal and trim off any excess pastry.

Mix the egg yolk and sugar together and generously brush all over the pie. Place in the preheated oven and bake for 40–45 minutes until the pie is golden brown and bubbling. Leave to cool slightly, then serve.

Salted Caramel and Toffee Date Puddings

My work colleague and good friend Mike Sunley would sometimes ask for this when he was in the restaurant. One day the mixture wasn't right – it was overcooked and chewy, yet we foolishly served it. To this day, some 15 years later, I'm still getting grief whenever we see it on any menu! This is for you Mike!

makes **10**

130g unsalted butter, plus 10g for greasing
350g soft dark brown muscovado sugar
3 large free-range eggs
450g plain flour, sifted
1 tablespoon baking powder
250g Medjool/toffee dates, stones removed and finely chopped
10 tablespoons Glittered Salted Caramel (see page 149)

Preheat the oven to 170°C/ Gas mark 3½. Butter ten 225ml metal dariole pudding moulds.

Cream the butter and sugar in a mixer with a paddle on a medium setting until light and fluffy. Gradually add the eggs, scraping down the sides of the bowl every now and again until mixed, then slowly fold in the flour and baking powder, and finally the chopped dates.

Spoon a tablespoon of salted caramel into each mould, then fill three-quarters full with the pudding mixture (this is a firm mix so it can also be rolled into balls and dropped into each mould).

Cover the top of each mould with a piece of buttered foil, then place in a roasting tray a quarter full of water (bain-marie) and bake for around 45–60 minutes. To check that the puddings are done, insert a wooden skewer into the centre – if it comes out clean, they are ready.

Allow to rest for a few minutes, turn out and serve with clotted cream or quality vanilla ice cream.

Coconut Straws and Dark Chocolate Dunk

An easy peasy pud or perfect with coffee. My big cheffy mate Andrew Turner used to serve a very refined version in his restaurant, mine are like me – rough, ready and rustic! Enjoy...

makes **20**

250g shop-bought puff pastry
plain flour, for dusting
1 egg yolk
50g soft desiccated coconut
150g good-quality dark chocolate

Line a baking tray with baking parchment.

Roll the puff pastry out on a floured work surface to measure 20 x 20cm, with a thickness of 5mm, then cut into strips 1cm wide.

Beat the egg yolk and brush over the pastry strips, then sprinkle over the desiccated coconut. Place on the lined baking tray 5mm apart and allow to rest in the fridge for 30 minutes.

Preheat the oven to 170C/ Gas mark 3½.

Place the baking tray in the preheated oven and bake for 12–15 minutes until golden brown.

Carefully melt the chocolate in a microwave or in a bowl over a pan of boiling water until shiny and glossy.

Serve the coconut straws in a jam jar with another jam jar filled with chocolate sauce for dipping.

"An easy peasy pud or perfect with coffee."

Willy Wonka's Chocolate Box

Both big and small will love these! Allow the chocolate in the piping bag to cool a little as this makes it slightly thicker and easier to pipe.

makes **18**

100g each of milk chocolate, dark chocolate and white chocolate
20g dried cranberries
20g dried apricots, chopped
40g peeled pistachios, chopped
edible gold dust
18 wooden skewers

Melt the milk, dark and white chocolate in 3 separate bowls set over pans of simmering water until silky and smooth. Remove from the heat and allow to cool slightly (around 5–10 minutes).

Line a baking tray with baking parchment. Place the wooden sticks on the silicone paper 7cm apart. Pour the melted chocolate into 3 piping bags (disposable ones are best) and trim the end with a pair of scissors so the chocolate pours out in a thin, consistent line.

Pipe chocolate circles over each skewer again and again until you've got a perfect lollipop. Make sure the wooden skewers are in the centre of the circles and well covered with chocolate. You should be able to make a minimum of 18 lollipops. Before the chocolate sets, sprinkle with the cranberries, apricots, chopped pistachios and edible gold.

Chill the tray of lollipops in the fridge. When they have set, gently peel the baking parchment off each lollipop.

"Both big and small will love these!"

Imani's Jaw-Sticking Peanut Butter Fudge

Lots of people struggle with making fudge, but this recipe is great and amazingly easy. The peanut butter gives it a really smooth texture and the sea salt kicks off a salt and sweet explosion. As when making a great risotto, stand over the saucepan slowly stirring and don't walk away – the 15 minutes it takes to cook is a great investment of time! Once cooled, the fudge can go into the fridge or store in a lidded container, if it lasts that long!

makes **16–20** *squares*

397g tin condensed milk
150ml double cream
450g demerara sugar
115g butter
2 tablespoons smooth peanut butter
1 teaspoon coarse sea salt, for sprinkling

Line a 20 x 20cm baking tin with baking parchment.

Place all ingredients apart from the salt in a heavy-based saucepan, bring to the boil, then turn down the heat and simmer for 10–15 minutes, stirring continuously.

If you have a sugar thermometer, this should read 115°C (soft ball stage); otherwise drop a small ball of the mixture into a bowl of iced water and see if it produces a soft ball.

Remove the saucepan from the heat and beat for 3–4 minutes until thick. The fudge will set as it cools, so while it is still slightly warm and fluid, pour it into the lined baking tin.

Finish with a sprinkle of salt, allow to cool and cut into squares.

"The peanut butter gives it a really smooth texture and the sea salt kicks off a salt and sweet explosion."

The Family Kitchen

Sparkling Barbie Turkish Delight

If you don't like rose Turkish delight, change the rose water to orange blossom water.
Try rolling the Turkish delight in pistachio dust (very finely chopped pistachios) and icing sugar for something a little more classic.

makes **25** *squares*

8 leaves of gelatine
500g caster sugar
4–6 drops rose water
4 drops of red food colouring
2 tablespoons cornflour
2 tablespoons icing sugar
1 teaspoon edible pink glitter
   (optional)

Line a 20 x 20 x 4cm dish with clingfilm.

Soak the gelatine leaves in cold water to soften (around 5 minutes).

Measure 400ml water into a saucepan and warm gently over a low heat.

Squeeze the excess water from the softened gelatine, then slowly stir it into the saucepan and let it dissolve. Stir in the caster sugar and allow to dissolve, then stir in the rose water and enough red food colouring to get a light pink colour. Pour into the lined dish and place in the fridge until set.

Once set, turn out and gently peel off the clingfilm, then cut into squares using a warm, sharp knife.

Mix the cornflour, icing sugar and edible glitter together, then roll the Turkish delight in the mixture.

Coconut Ice

A real old-school sweet recipe which is very easy to make. This is a dry mix, but if you like your coconut ice a bit stickier, add an extra splash of condensed milk.

makes **20–30** *squares*

500g icing sugar
397g tin condensed milk
400g desiccated coconut
1 vanilla pod, seeds reserved
red food colouring
$\frac{1}{2}$ teaspoon edible pink glitter

Line a 20 x 20cm baking tin with clingfilm.

Sift the icing sugar into a large bowl, add the condensed milk, coconut and vanilla seeds, then mix well with gloved hands (this mix will be dry and tight so you really have to get stuck in).

Divide the mixture in half. Press one half into the bottom of the tin in an even layer.

Add a few drops of red food colouring to the remaining half and mix until the colour has been evenly distributed. Carefully spread and press the pink mix on top of the white to form an even layer.

Place in the fridge to set for 2 hours, then sprinkle with edible glitter, cut into squares and serve.

Nut Brittle

You won't be able to leave this alone, but watch out for those fillings!

serves **4**

300g caster sugar
2 tablespoons liquid glucose
75g unsalted peanuts
75g unsalted cashews
50g shelled pistachios
25g sesame seeds

Line a baking tray with baking parchment.

Pour the sugar and glucose into a heavy-based saucepan and place over a low heat, do not stir. When the sugar and glucose have dissolved, increase the heat and cook until you have a nice golden brown caramel.

Add in all the remaining ingredients and stir quickly, then pour out onto the lined tray. Try to get a nice even layer of brittle. Leave to set and go cold, then use a rolling pin or a hammer to smash into pieces.

Pistachio Drop Meringues

makes **16–18**

4 medium egg whites
240g caster sugar, plus extra for dusting
20g pistachios, peeled and chopped

Preheat the oven to 140°C/ Gas mark 1. Line a baking tray with baking parchment and dust with a little caster sugar.

Whisk the egg whites in a food mixer until they form soft peaks. Continue whisking and slowly add half the sugar, making sure it is thoroughly incorporated into the egg whites.

Remove the bowl from the mixer and very slowly fold in the rest of the sugar by hand using a large metal spoon. You should end up with a raw meringue that is thick and silky in texture and has a glossy sheen.

Using a tablespoon, drop spoonfuls of the meringue onto the lined baking tray and dust with the chopped pistachios. Bake in the preheated oven for 30–40 minutes or until they lift easily off the baking parchment.

The Family Kitchen

Index

Thank you

Wow, where do I start? From the beginning I suppose!

So to my wonderful, stable family life, with my lovely wife Amber steering the family ship with all my lovely children, thank you.

The book was a real challenge to put together, especially when it came to looming deadlines, and there is absolutely no way I would have or could have got it all off the ground without the support of two people who helped put down all the behind-the-scenes work. Emma Rogers, who helped with Cook with Kids and now The Family Kitchen – you made sense of all my handwritten scraps of paper and spent countless hours formatting with me! Over these two books I've seen Emma go from strength to strength and she is now on her way to becoming a shining star in our industry. On to a top chef and friend, David Steel – a truly gifted guy who unselfishly parted with recipes, helped write others and tested a lot of the dishes in this book. David, you're a true Trojan who gave me belief when work and home-life pressures were bearing down. An unsung hero in every way.

Behind those guys are Lexington Superstar Chefs – Simon Merrick and Daryl Young. Thanks for nights and days of trialling in between your everyday kitchen lives, and for a lot of ducking and diving!

Lara Holmes totally understands and gets the Kirby family. She is a true friend and a hugely talented photographer who I believe is one of the country's best. We worked together on my first book and it's fair to say there is a kind of magic that happens. Lastly, enter the third musketeer, the very lovely Katie Cecil, prop and 'food stylist from the gods'. Truly talented with an unbelievable eye for style and beauty, we styled the food together with ease. This completes the dream team. The photography took place over an emotional week and I hope this shows through in the book. It has put down a foundation of friendship and I can't wait to work together again.

It's like an addiction! It was a real honour to work with you both.

My friend and publisher Jon Croft and art director Matt Inwood, who kept us all on track without shouting or clipping our creative wings. Matt, you are a true star and responsible for the quirky and fun and edgy front page and the amazing look and feel of this book. Also, editor Gillian Haslam who, from afar, has been amazing, polite and patient along the journey!

Lastly, my good friends and work colleagues in this amazing, wonderful industry, particularly Mike Sunley who has been a colleague, friend and rock of support, who gives counsel in my work and sometimes home life, even when I don't want to hear it! Gregg Wallace, for the heartfelt foreword – you are a true mate who has made it to the big league but who hasn't forgotten us all. Thank you for being a loyal and honest mate. 'Finally', I hear you cry!

And back to what this book is all about – my lovely, beautiful family of Amber, Tabitha, Jasper and Imani. Thank you x

Thank you

Rob Kirby

Rob Kirby is a Master Chef of Great Britain and also a fellow and active member of the highly esteemed Royal Academy of Culinary Arts.

With over 30 years of kitchen experience, Rob has cooked in the finest hotels, restaurants and also personally for profile clients and members of the Royal family at various times throughout those years, both in the UK and abroad. He is now a director of the highly successful top-end catering company, Lexington.

His first book, *Cook With Kids*, achieved worldwide success and won 'Best Fund Raising Charity and Community Cookbook in Europe' at the World Gourmand Cookbook Awards in Paris. It also featured in the *Independent* newspaper's 'Top 10 Children's Cookbooks'.

Rob appears regularly on television and radio throughout the year, including every Christmas Day over the last decade showing the nation how to cook their turkey!

He is a huge supporter of the school at Great Ormond Street Hospital to which shared monies and royalties will go from the sale of this book, as they did with his first book.